OUT OF THE Fishbowl

Choosing a route less traveled

A Memoir by
Ken Miller

Trafford
PUBLISHING™

Order this book online at www.trafford.com/06-0116
or email orders@trafford.com

Most Trafford titles are also available at major online book retailers.

Note for Librarians: A cataloguing record for this book is available from Library
and Archives Canada at www.collectionscanada.ca/amicus/index-e.html

Printed in Victoria, BC, Canada.

ISBN: 978-1-4120-8361-4

*We at Trafford believe that it is the responsibility of us all, as both individuals
and corporations, to make choices that are environmentally and socially sound.
You, in turn, are supporting this responsible conduct each time you purchase a
Trafford book, or make use of our publishing services. To find out how you are
helping, please visit www.trafford.com/responsiblepublishing.html*

*Our mission is to efficiently provide the world's finest, most comprehensive
book publishing service, enabling every author to experience success.
To find out how to publish your book, your way, and have it available
worldwide, visit us online at www.trafford.com/10510*

 www.trafford.com

North America & international
toll-free: 1 888 232 4444 (USA & Canada)
phone: 250 383 6864 ♦ fax: 250 383 6804 ♦ email: info@trafford.com

The United Kingdom & Europe
phone: +44 (0)1865 722 113 ♦ local rate: 0845 230 9601
facsimile: +44 (0)1865 722 868 ♦ email: info.uk@trafford.com

10 9 8 7 6 5 4 3 2

About the Cover

After John brought me the first set of cover illustrations for this book and I fell in love with the magnified images being displayed on my CCTV, it occurred to me that many who will read this book may be reading it via cassette tape, internet connection, Talking Book Radio or some other electronic format and will therefore miss the fun cover. So, if I may, let me describe it for you.

Aside from the title, two main elements make up the cover: A fish bowl and a fish.

The fish bowl, on the left side of the cover, along with the usual stuff you'd find in a fish bowl, has two fish looking to the right with big eyes and shocked expressions on their faces. One even has a fin over its mouth as if to say, "Oh, no. You can't do that!" The water has been disturbed and some is spilling over the left side of the bowl. The spilled water forms "fin prints" that go to the right side of the cover and lead to a fish walking away from the fish bowl wearing dark glasses and holding a white cane in its right fin. A delightful smirk on the face of the fish completes the picture: the fish is free! It's out of the fish bowl.

To Kathy
who, in 1972, suffered
a momentary lapse
in good judgment
and said: "I do."

Contents

Introduction

The slamming screen door and screeching kids' Keds on the kitchen floor announced my arrival. "Mom, everybody's riding their bikes to first grade. Can I ride mine, too?"

"I'm in the living room, honey. What did you say?"

A few more steps and I was on the carpet. "Everybody's riding their bikes to school. Can I ride mine, too?"

The living room was quiet. I wasn't sure if she had heard me so I was about to repeat myself when she spoke. "I think we should wait until your dad gets home. I'll talk it over with him when I pick him up at the depot. His train will be here in just a few minutes."

"He wants to what?" Dad laughed and took off his engineer's cap, tossing it into the back seat as he got into the car.

"He wants to ride his bike to school."

"That's ridiculous. Riding around our neighborhood on the sidewalks is one thing, but out on the streets? He could get hit by a car! He could get killed! It's too dangerous; I don't think he should do it."

"I know, I agree," she said. "It would be much too dangerous. So..." she paused. "Do you want to be the one to tell him he can't?"

He turned to face her. "No, I don't want to tell him. Do you?"

"No, I was hoping you would."

It was quiet inside the car while they thought about what to do. Mom broke the silence. "How about this? We have another eye appointment in a couple of weeks, let's let Dr. Martens tell him."

Chapter 1

To See, Or Not To See

What can he see? What can't he see? Those were the questions my folks wrestled with for the first few years of my life.

It all started on Easter Sunday morning, 1952. I was six months old and had just finished breakfast. Standing five feet from my high chair, Mom opened a shopping bag and pulled out a brightly colored rabbit. "Hopping" it around the counter top, she called to me "Kenny, look who's here!" Her voice was full of enthusiasm. I turned my head in her direction, but didn't respond to her question or the colorful bouncing rabbit. Still excited she spoke again "Kenny, look who's come to see you!" She made the rabbit jump a little higher, causing its long ears to flop from side to side. Once again I leaned forward in my chair with an expressionless face and made no response.

The next time she spoke her voice was stressed. Her encouraging, playful tone had been replaced by a tense urgency. Her words were no longer a call to fun; they were a command to action. "Kenny, look at the rabbit!" Again, I turned my head in her direction, leaned forward and squinted.

Moments later, in their bedroom, Dad tried to calm her fears by reminding her that no one else in the family had eye problems. He told her my lack of interest in the rabbit must be caused by something else. Through her tears, she hoped he was right.

Mom didn't know what to think. Most of the time, I gave no indication that I had difficulty seeing. When another family would come to visit, I'd sit on the floor and play with the toys just like the other kids. Before I went to bed at night, I'd sit on Mom's lap and we would look at my picture books. Opening the book, Mom would ask: "Where is the ball?" I'd pointed to it quickly. "Where is the cute little kitty?" Again, I would point to the kitty in the picture.

As time went on it became more obvious to everyone that I had a real problem. Even our black lab, Prince, sensed that something was wrong.

Our house was on Seventh Street between Highway 10 and Third Avenue. Every time I went outside to ride my tricycle Prince would go with me. He ran along side me as I raced down the sidewalk toward the busy highway. When I got close to the end of the sidewalk, He stood in my way, forcing me to stop. Then I'd turn around and go in the other direction. Prince would run with me to the other end of the sidewalk and block my way once again.

When I was about two and a half years old my folks decided to take me to an eye specialist. Dr. Lund, our family doctor, made an appointment for us in St. Cloud, about a two hour drive from home.

After a short question-answer period with my folks, the doctor took a box that sat next to his desk and placed it in front of me. It was filled with blocks. Each one was a different shape and size. I would learn later that they also were of different colors. He watched and took some notes as I played with the blocks. Then he pulled out an eye chart for children. Instead of letters, it had pictures on it.

He sat across the room from me and kept asking me questions about the chart. I didn't respond to any of them. I continued to play with the blocks that were in front of me. When he finished the exam, he turned to my parents.

"Mr. and Mrs. Miller," he began slowly, "your son is almost blind. Even though he has a little sight, for all practical purposes, he *is* blind and will probably be blind for the rest of his life."

Deep down inside they suspected something had to be wrong. Nevertheless, to hear someone actually say the word out loud was like a blow from the blacksmith's hammer. Their unspoken fear was a reality.

After a short pause, he continued "I don't know the reason for his blindness but would like to do exploratory surgery to see what I can find."

Surgery? Just to explore? Mom's eyes burned and the thought of her son being operated on--just to explore: was unthinkable! No, it was absolutely out of the question!

10

Then the voice of reason spoke: What if it would help? What if they were able to correct his blindness? This could be his lifetime ticket into a sighted world. Not going with the surgery may deny him his sight.

Reluctantly, with many mixed emotions, they scheduled a day for me to have the surgery.

Dazed by the reality of having a blind son and fearful of the upcoming surgery, Mom held me tight on her lap and wept during the entire trip home.

As soon as they arrived in Staples, they contacted Dr. Lund and let him know what had happened. He told them to get a second opinion as soon as possible. "I'm concerned that the surgery is too risky," he said. "First, even if the doctors find the cause of Kenny's blindness, there is no guarantee it could be corrected. Second, is the very real possibility that, if the surgery is unsuccessful, Kenny could lose what little sight he has."

Unwilling to take such risks, my parents cancelled the exploratory surgery.

The doctor they chose for the second opinion was an eye specialist in St. Paul.

We were seated in the waiting room when a nurse came through a side door and talked to my parents. She told them that I needed to have my eyes dilated with eye drops before the exam. Dilating my eyes, she explained, would open the pupils so the doctor could get a better view of their interior. I sat on Mom's lap and tilted my head back while the nurse put one, two, three of the drops of cold liquid into each eye.

Twenty minutes later my name was called and the nurse took us to a smaller office where we waited for the doctor. Mom and Dad sat down and I scrambled to get back onto Mom's lap.

When the doctor entered the office he spoke to my parents, and then asked me if he could look in my eyes. Pulling a small flashlight from his pocket, he began the exam.

As the doctor explored my right eye, then my left, he uttered an occasional "hmm" and "uh-huh."

Still inspecting, he spoke to my parents. "Everything looks fine so far—cornea, pupil, iris, retina...." then his voice trailed off.

"What is it, doctor?" Mom asked.

"I'm looking at the optic nerve," he explained." I can see it at the point where it attaches to the retina." He hesitated, shining the light in just one spot, first in the right, then the left, "It is dull white." He switched off the light and turned to my parents.

11

"I don't understand," said Mom.

"It should be healthy pink."

"What does that mean?"

"The dull color means the nerves are almost dead. It means that Kenny's blindness is caused by a nerve problem, not an eye problem. He has optic atrophy. His eyes receive and process information just like yours and mine. Unfortunately, almost all of that information is lost by the nerve before it reaches his brain. It's a bit like the headlights on a car. They may be fine, the battery may be good, but if the wires that connect the two are broken or corroded, the lights won't work properly."

"Does that mean that eye surgery or eye transplants would be unnecessary?"

"Totally unnecessary. His eyes are fine. Why replace them? It's the nerves that need to be replaced."

Mom and Dad breathed a unified sigh of relief as they realized that their decision to cancel my "exploratory surgery" had been the right one.

"Where do we go to get a nerve transplant?"

"That type of surgery has not yet been developed. Frankly, the possibility of it even being developed is very remote. It would involve the eye, the nerve and the brain. The optic nerve is about the size of a pencil in diameter. It contains thousands of little fibers that carry information from the eye to the brain. To successfully disconnect the unhealthy nerve from the eye and brain and then transplant a healthy nerve in its place would be a real miracle. At this point in history, medical science is not even close to performing an operation of that complexity. I'm sorry."

"Is there anything we can do?"

"No. Mrs. Miller, your son is functionally blind. There is nothing that can be done."

"What about his future?"

"My recommendation would be for you to institutionalize him."

What? Mom couldn't believe her ears. What is he saying? Institutionalize my son? No way! In her heart she gritted her teeth and made a decision. "Kenny didn't need surgery—and he won't be institutionalized, either!"

Being Christians and having a strong faith in God, they sought a miracle through Kathryn Kuhlmans' healing ministry. Mom wrote her a letter explaining our situation and asked for prayer. In response, Kathryn sent a very kind letter and a prayer cloth. The cloth came with a brief note of instruction:

"Tonight, place this cloth across your son's eyes after he is asleep. In the morning when he wakes up, he will be healed."

After I was asleep, Mom tip-toed into my room and laid the cloth over my eyes. Her heart was filled with anticipation and excitement. She could hardly wait until morning. At last, her son would be able to see!

Rushing into my room the next day she found me playing with my stuffed rabbit, the crumpled cloth at the foot of my bed.

I was three and a half years old on our first visit to the Mayo Clinic. Appointments were scheduled over a six day period with pediatricians, neurologists and a team of eye specialists.

After all the tests were completed, my folks met with the doctors to go over the results. Those from the pediatricians indicated that I was in good health. The neurologist reported the results of their test were within normal range for a child my age. Eye specialist, Dr. Christoferson, confirmed what they had already been told: I had optic atrophy. My optic nerves were the source of my blindness, not my eyes. He did make this comment on his written report regarding numbers to assign for my vision: "Difficult to obtain because of lack of cooperation..." (Hey, I was only three!)

My folks decided that it would be a good idea to continue visiting the Mayo clinic once a year. Those visits would keep them abreast of any medical advances, and the exams would alert them to any changes in my vision. Dr. Martens was the specialist we saw each summer through my junior high years.

Another lively game of Simon Says was over. Neighborhood moms were calling kids home for bedtime snack. "Hey, Kenny!" David called to me as he sped away on his bike. "Ask your mom if you can ride your bike to school."

The slamming screen door and screeching kids' Keds on the kitchen floor announced my arrival. "Mom, everybody's riding their bikes to first grade. Can I ride mine, too?"

"I'm in the living room, honey. What did you say?"

A few more steps and I was on the carpet. "Everybody's riding their bikes to school. Can I ride mine, too?"

The living room was quiet.. I wasn't sure if she had heard me so I was about to repeat myself when she spoke. "I think we should wait until your dad gets home. I'll talk it over with him when I pick him up at the depot."

"He wants to what?" Dad laughed and took off his engineer's cap, tossing it into the back seat as he got into the car.

"He wants to ride his bike to school."

"That's ridiculous. Riding around our neighborhood on the sidewalks is one thing, but out on the streets? He could get hit by a car! He could get killed! It's too dangerous; I don't think he should do it."

"I know, I agree," she said. "It would be much too dangerous. So..." she paused. "Do you want to be the one to tell him he can't? He really has his heart set on it."

He turned to face her. "No, I don't want to tell him. Do you?"

"No, I was hoping you would."

It was quiet inside the car while they thought about what to do. Mom broke the silence. "How about this? We have another eye appointment in a couple of weeks, let's let Dr. Martens tell him."

Before checking in, we had time to pick up some new shoes for me to wear to First Grade, and catch a quick lunch.

Sitting in the back seat, with the window rolled down, I could smell, and almost taste the greasy cheese burger and crispy fries that I had ordered. Then I heard her voice; it sounded like she was talking to me.

"Well, hello there, young man, you look like you're waiting for lunch." Her voice was kind and genuine.

"Yes, I am"

"And what are you going to have?"

"A cheese burger, fries and a root beer!"

"Oh boy, that sounds yummy! Do you like lots of ketchup with your fries?"

"Do I ever!"

"Me too, and lots of ice in my pop!"

"Yeah!"

"Mmm..., I'm gettin' hungry just thinkin' about it! Hey, it looks like my order is ready; I must go. It has been very nice talking with you. Bye for now."

Her footsteps crunched as she crossed the gravel parking lot to her car.

When I heard her car door close, I directed my attention to the front seat of our car.

"She was really pretty wasn't she, Mom?"

Having observed the woman's unkempt hair, weathered face and tattered dress, she hesitated, then said, "Yes, honey, she was."

Squinting through dilated eyes, I climbed up into the exam chair to wait for Dr. Martens. I could smell that new shoe smell from my Buster Browns and wondered if my Keds wouldn't be a better choice for my bike rides to school.

Just then the door opened. "Hello, Kenny. How are you today?" After shaking my hand, which I thought was pretty cool, he sat down and the exam began.

The wheels of his chair squeaked as he rolled it in front of me and gave me a plastic card.

"Kenny, can you identify any of the letters on this card?"

Examining the card, I didn't see anything that looked like a letter, just some little shapeless smears.

Making another attempt, I concentrated real hard, held the card close to my face and strained to focus my eyes. No matter what I did, I could only recognize one thing on that plastic card. His Old Spice.

"Let's try counting fingers." He stepped away from me perhaps ten feet, and stretched out his hand. "Can you tell me how many fingers I am holding out, Kenny?"

I could hardly tell that he had even moved his arm, let alone count fingers! He took one step toward me and held out his hand.

"Four." He was holding up three.

"How about now?" he took a step closer and held up two.

"One."

"How about now?"

"Five." He was holding up four.

"Let's try again." He took another step toward me and held out three fingers. At this point, his hand was two feet away from the end of my nose.

"Three!"

"Excellent! Now how many?"

"Four"

"Excellent!"

I felt pretty good about being able to count fingers at two feet since I had not done well with the eye chart.

"Okay, let's try reading the chart with this pair of glasses." They felt cold and heavy as he set them on my nose and hooked them behind my ears.

Again, the wheels of his chair let me know he was moving. This time it was to what appeared to me to be a big dark cabinet. Opening the door, he chose several lenses and returned to me.

Inserting a lens into the glasses and giving me the eye chart, he asked if I could recognize anything on the card. The blotches, that I assumed were letters, were a little more focused than before, but still not focused enough to be identified.

Next, he tried several types of prescription lenses to see if they would help, even just a little. They didn't. Looking through the prescription lenses only distorted the image I was looking at. It was like trying to read through an ice cube!

Next we started experimenting with magnifying lenses. We tried four, five, maybe six different lenses, each with increasing powers of magnification. I noticed that each time the level of magnification was increased, the card had to be held closer to my eyes to keep it in focus. I also noticed that, as the magnification increased, my viewing area decreased.

With the first lens I tried, I kept the card in focus by holding it a foot from my face. The image was in focus, but unreadable. By the time we had reached the last lens I had the card right on the end of my nose. I felt a bit self-conscious about the way I must have looked, but the card was in focus and I could identify all four of the letters I saw through the lens! It was wonderful! The key to my being able to read was magnification, lots of magnification.

"Doctor," Mom spoke, "what could have happened to his optic nerves?"

"It's hard to say. The damage may have been caused by a difficult birth or severe trauma to the head."

"Yes," Mom offered, "his birth was extremely difficult. I was in labor with him for forty hours. I am built so small that I couldn't deliver him. Finally, the doctor used forceps. I couldn't see him right away and when I did, his head was covered with a blanket. Only his face was visible. It was only after we had taken him home that we discovered the scabs on his head from the forceps."

"His optic nerves could have been injured at that time."

"Will his vision get worse?"

"No, I don't think so. The condition of the nerves seems to be stable. It shouldn't change. As he gets older, Kenny will be subject to the same changes in his eyes that we all experience, but the condition of his nerves will stay the same."

"If twenty–twenty is perfect vision, what is Kenny's?"

"It would be about 20/400."

"What does that mean?"

"It means what a person with normal vision sees at four hundred feet, Kenny would see at twenty feet."

She swallowed to clear the lump in her throat before asking the next question.

"What about school? Must we institutionalize him?"

"Heavens no, keep him at home. I know a number of children with low vision like Kenny's. They live at home and do very well in public school. You may want to get in touch with State Services for the Blind. They can be very helpful."

Thinking the exam was over, I jumped down from the chair and headed for the door.

"Wait a minute, Kenny. We have one more question to ask the doctor." I stopped and turned to face them, wondering what the question was. Then I remembered.

"What do you think about Kenny riding his bike to school?"

· The room was silent. Then he spoke. "Why not? You can't keep him in a fish bowl forever."

Chapter 2

———————

Life in the Fast Lane

People in Staples thought my folks were nuts to let me ride a bike. Great-aunt Adeline was one of them. Each time she'd see me on my red Schwinn going downtown with some other kids, she'd get on the phone to Mom. "Donna, you're crazy to let that boy ride a bike! He just about got hit by a car in front of my house!" There never was traffic in front of Aunt Ad's place. If there was, I would have heard it.

Preparing me for bike rides to school, I was given two parental admonitions. First, "Watch out for cars!" which I interpreted as "Listen for cars." Second, "Only cross Highway 10 at the stoplight." At that time, the only reason for crossing Highway 10 was to get to Perry's Ben Franklin. That's where the candy was and candy was important.

Usually when I went downtown, I just did what the other kids did. If they stopped, I'd stop. If they kept going, I'd keep going. However there were times that I would have to make a "candy run" by myself.

On my first solo trip downtown, I stopped at the corner of Fourth Street and Highway 10, squinted and searched the opposite side of the road for the stop light that had to be there. Nope, no stop light, just a nose full of exhaust from the car idling to my left.

What about the color of the light next to me? Reaching out to the round coolness of the light pole and straining on tip-toe, my eyes followed the straight pole up, up, up, into nothing. Just then the idling car shifted gears and sped across the highway leaving me with another nose full of exhaust and a question: Can moving cars tell me when it's safe to cross the highway?

If the car beside me was waiting to go, it could be assumed that the light was yellow or red. If, on the other hand, the cars to my left were crossing the highway, it could be assumed the light was green or yellow. Waiting for the lights to cycle before crossing was the way I avoided getting caught in the intersection because of a short yellow light. Allowing the lights to cycle may have taken a minute or two, but starting across the highway on a fresh green light made me feel safe and secure.

If there were no lights at the intersection, I'd slow down and listen very carefully. Listening would let me know about oncoming traffic. Slowing my speed would make it easier to stop if necessary.

Along with determining stop light color, one other adjustment to my bicycle riding needed to be made. It may seem unsafe and risky, but for a bicyclist who listens more than looks, it works very well. I liked to ride in the traffic lane rather than near the curb. The area between the curb and traffic lane could have all sorts of dangerous stuff lying in it: quiet stuff like rocks, sticks, storm sewer covers, loose gravel and the worst hazard of them all—a parked car! At least a moving vehicle makes noise so you can get out of its way. A rock just lies there waiting for some innocent bike rider to hit it.

My Cub Scout meeting was over and if I hurried home, I'd have time to watch my favorite cartoon show," Yogi Bear". Flying up the driveway and slowing to enter the garage, I lowered the kick stand and parked my bike. After taking two giant steps up the three stairs to the back door, I paused to pet Prince before going into the house.

Why he was always curled up, sleeping on that little landing was a mystery to me. How could he get any rest? Every time someone needed to use the back door, he would have to wake up and move!

And if that weren't annoying enough, the chain between his dog house and collar was so short that it wouldn't lie flat on the ground when he was on the landing. When he would lie down, it would hang there, suspended four inches off the ground. The chain spanned the entire width of our garage. From the dog house it passed Dad's work bench, then the garbage cans, then the door that led to the back yard, and finally, it rose to meet his collar.

From inside the house I could hear the TV, "Mr. Ranger isn't gonna like this, Yogi." I gave Prince one more scratch behind his ear and then hurried to my viewing position two feet in front of the TV.

When the show was almost over, I heard Mom call from the kitchen, "Kenny, would you go find your brother and tell him that supper is almost ready? He is playing in the yard somewhere."

"Okay." I didn't jump up at that very moment; I waited until the last musical note was finished after they had rolled the credits.

Making up for lost time, I kicked it into high gear and rushed out the front door. Standing on the top step, I yelled: "Doug, where are you?" All was quiet; that meant he had to be in the back.

The fastest way to get to the back yard from the front steps was through the garage. I flew down the steps, rounded the corner into the garage, burned up the concrete floor heading straight for the back door right past the sleeping Prince.

The next thing I remember was the feel of a cold wash cloth on my very sensitive head and hearing my dad's voice. "Are you okay? You got yourself a real goose egg that time."

Lifting a tentative hand, I explored the stinging lump above my right eye. Yes indeed, it was shaped like an egg. Mom told me it was going to turn some pretty impressive shades of black and blue.

Supper didn't sound good. All I wanted to do was to lie on the couch and hold the cold cloth to my aching head. Cinder, our chubby Chihuahua, jumped up on the couch and licked my face. From the other end of the living room I could hear the TV: "Good night, Chet. Good night David. And good night for NBC News."

We bought a longer chain for Prince, and I was back on my bike the next day.

Standing in the doorway, I heard something go "clack." Then, another clack. The sound came from the front of my Sunday school classroom. On the way to investigate, I heard the voice of my teacher.

"Hi, Kenny."

"Hi, Mrs. Peterson."

"I'm just setting up the easel for our new flannel graph."

"What's a flannel graph?"

"It will help me tell our Bible story for today. Would you like to see how it works?"

I walked over to where she stood.

"In front of you on the table are the paper cut- outs of the characters in the story."

I picked up one of the cut outs. It seemed to be about eight or nine inches tall and cut in the shape of a person with a head on top and feet on the bottom. One side was paper and had a picture on it. The other side felt soft, like my pajamas.

"That's Jesus," she said, "In the story today, He is going to meet a blind man." Pausing for a moment, she moved the cut outs around on the table and pulled one from the pile. Handing me another cut out, she explained: "This is the blind man when he is sitting by the roadside begging."

The paper that she handed me was shaped like a triangle with rounded edges. I guessed the edges must have been his head and knees.

"During the story," she continued, "these cut outs will stick to the flannel on the board. As the story changes, I can switch the cut outs around, like this." She took Jesus from my hand and put Him on the board, then took the blind man and put him next to Jesus.

"In the story, Jesus heals the blind man and he can see." Again, she moved some of the cut outs on the table and handed me another. This one was taller than the Jesus figure that I had held moments earlier. This guy's arms were in the air above his head like he was reaching for the sky. His legs were far apart as if he were jumping. "The man is so happy that he jumps into the air and runs to tell his family and friends that he can see!"

Our case worker told us about a weekend event that would be held at a place called Camp Courage. "Normally," she explained, "the camps are for people with physical disabilities, but this one will be for parents and their blind or visually impaired children. It would be a great opportunity for Kenny to meet other blind kids and for you both to meet parents with blind children."

When we arrived, the parking lot was buzzing with activity. Parents, kids and luggage were everywhere. After we got settled in our room, we went to the recreation hall to meet some of the other campers. Walking through the door, we were confronted by a wall of noise and laughter. Games had been organized and it sounded like everyone was having a good time.

Being the only blind kid in Staples, this was a new experience for me and my folks. Not knowing what to do, we located a table and sat down.

My parents watched the way other parents related to their children. Some were extremely protective, not letting the child off their laps. Others were encouraging their children to explore the world around them.

At the table next to us, a boy was speaking to his mom.

"I'm thirsty," he said.

"There's a water fountain straight across the room from us. It's on the wall past the tables. You can make the trip easily."

His cane grazed the leg of my chair as he began his journey. Then I heard furniture legs scrape the floor as he bumped into something. His parents, only a few feet away, remained seated, quietly watching. Pausing for a moment and then giving the floor a couple of taps, he continued his trip to the water fountain.

The next day, while our parents were in meetings, some of us went on a pontoon boat ride on the lake.

The sun was warm as we stepped from the dock onto the boat. This was my first pontoon boat ride and I wanted to enjoy everything about it. Sitting on a wooden bench in the back, I was flooded with new sensations. From the rumbling vibrations of the motor to the scented mixture of gasoline and suntan lotion, to the refreshing spray from the churning water and the occasional whiff of fish decomposing on some distant shore. I loved it all.

After we had been on the lake for a while, some of the kids started talking to one another. One conversation between two girls caught my attention. It had to do with "lights out".

"How late did you stay up last night?"

"Two o'clock," She snickered. "I couldn't stop reading. My book was really funny!"

"Yup, mine, too. When they said, 'lights out' I just put my book under the covers and kept reading."

One of the speakers in a general session said something that my folks memorized and put into practice. "In all your decisions related to your child remember: If you treat him like a handicapped child, he will grow up to be a handicapped adult. If you treat him like a 'normal' child, he will grow up to be a normal adult."

It was useless to resist. The warm summer sun, the smell of freshly cut grass, birds singing in the trees, coins in my pocket, candy at the Ben Franklin and my bike only a few feet away in the garage. That combination meant only one thing: take bike to get candy.

The stoplights were on my side and on the return trip the pockets of my shorts were bursting with a quarter's worth of licorice, Root Beer barrels, Chum-Gum, M&M's, Sweet Tarts and those little wax bottles filled with Kool-Aid.

Before going home, I planned to stop at Grandma's house. She lived half way between the Ben Franklin and my place. Stopping there would allow me time to eat most of the candy before Mom found out I had it, not because she didn't want me to have candy, but because she had a sweet tooth and I didn't want to share.

Fifth street from downtown to Grandma's house is a short trip of four blocks, all downhill. Riding downhill is great fun, especially with the wind at your back. On a good day, under the right conditions, breaking the sound barrier would not be unreasonable.

Standing at the top of the hill, I gave one last listen to see if any vehicles were in the area. The only sound was the rustle of the leaves in the trees. Jumping on my bike, I began my fearless flight to the bottom of the hill. The sun sizzled on the back of my neck as I pumped and pedaled until I thought I'd explode.

Warm summer air whipped past my face and tore at my hair. I was an eagle rocketing towards its prey! With teeth clenched and adrenaline pouring into my veins, my bike and I became one red hot flash as we screamed past the Mary Rondorf home and the Methodist church on our lightning swift journey to the bottom.

Through the handlebars I could feel my tires chewing up the pavement under me. I listened... I listened again. I heard nothing, not a sound behind me, not a sound in front of me. The road was mine, all mine! It was truly a great day to be alive! I went blasting past the huge Elm trees that lined the road "faster than a speeding bullet!" I was invincible! Nothing could stop me! Nothing could...

Without warning, my revelry was interrupted by an unfamiliar, new sensation. The eagle was no longer on his bike—he was air born and his wings weren't working! The flight was short, the landing a disaster.

Hitting the pavement and bouncing a couple times, I rolled to a stop. My shoulder, elbow and palms were bruised but the real damage was to my right knee. It was missing a round chunk of skin about the size of a fifty cent piece.

24

From my seated position, I squinted and scanned the road near me to see if I could find my bike. It was lying just a few feet away near the curb. Wondering what had stopped my flight, I stood to my feet and hobbled up the hill to see what I could find.

Five or six steps later, a dark shadow on the road caught my attention. Shaped like a football, the shadow belonged to a large rock. It was round and thick in the middle and pointed at the ends. How it got to that spot in the traffic lane was a mystery to me. I rolled it over to the curb, picked up my bike and limped the rest of the way to Grandma's house for some medical attention and some chocolate chip cookies.

Wincing each time she rubbed some of that stingy stuff on my knee, I patted my pockets because candy is important.

Chapter 3

———————

Workin' on the Railroad

We were just finishing supper when Dad asked me a question:

"Would you like to go to Dilworth with me on the train tonight? We'll leave in about an hour and won't be back until six or seven o'clock tomorrow morning."

"In the engine? In the front of the train?"

"Yes," his voice smiled. "In the engine. In the front of the train."

At school, our class had taken a field trip to Wadena, about seventeen miles from Staples, in a passenger car in the middle of the train. Riding in the engine, in the front, was something that never crossed my mind. Now it was going to happen. Finishing my supper with one giant gulp, I went to pack my "grip." That's what Dad called his little suitcase, so that's what I called mine.

Mom gave us a ride to the railroad yards and dropped Dad off at the depot. She said I should stay with her while Dad found out which train we would be on. Then he would signal us when it was time to go.

We parked between the "yards" and Wimpy's Cafe. The smell of greasy hamburgers drifted through the open car window as we waited for Dad's signal.

Only one engine was sitting in the "yard" but it rumbled like distant thunder. Feeling the ground tremble under its massive weight, I could almost see the huge puffs of black being forced from its smoke stack. On the other side of the "yards," by the "round house," came the crash and bang of box cars being slammed together forming another train.

"Okay, honey, it's time to go."

With my grip in hand and my blue and white striped engineer's cap on my head, I rushed toward the thundering black smudge that would take us to Dilworth. Each breath I took filled my nostrils with the thick smell of the creosote soaked railroad ties and the sweetness of the clover that grew along the tracks.

Dad was waiting for me and lifted me to the first step of the ladder leading into the engine. I could feel the deep vibrations of the huge machine as I climbed aboard.

Once inside the engine, I was greeted by the heavy aroma of diesel fuel. Straight ahead of me was an enormous glass water bottle that was sitting on a narrow stand. Dad pulled a paper cup from the dispenser on the wall and showed me how to get some water from the cooler.

Without warning a door at the back of the engine opened and a friendly voice spoke: "Hey, Pat. I see you've brought your assistant today."

Dad introduced me to the man who would be the fireman on our trip. After shaking his hand, Dad picked me up and set me on the engineer's chair.

"This is the throttle." He put my hand on a thick smooth lever to my right. "It controls how fast we go."

"Where is the steering wheel?"

"You don't need one in a train. It rides on the rails and goes wherever they go. Now up here, way above your head, is the handle you pull when you want to blow the whistle. The handle is on the end of a long rope..."

"Can I blow it?" I interrupted.

"Yes—but not now. You can blow it when we are on our way out of town. Right now I want you to wait here and I'll be right back. We have to check a few things before we go." Dad and the fireman went through a narrow door at the back of the engine. I successfully resisted the temptation to blow the whistle.

When they returned they sat in their chairs and the rumble grew louder. The powerful vibrations of the engine became more intense and soon we were moving. Not very fast at first, but we were moving!

The box cars behind us clanked and squeaked as we increased speed. Then I felt Dad's strong hands lifting me up so I could grab the handle to the whistle. I pulled on it, but it wouldn't blow. Then Dad let go of me. I hung there on the end of the rope like a monkey on a vine. I was pulling it with all my might and it finally blew!

It was past my bedtime when we arrived in Dilworth. I was enjoying the sounds and smells of my railroad adventure, but could hardly keep my eyes open.

We took a taxi to Moorhead, a town just a couple miles west of Dilworth, where the railroad was renting a sort of "bunk house" for its overnight crews. We opened the screen door but didn't turn on the light when we went inside. We didn't want to wake up any of the others who were sleeping, but the floor still creaked with each of our footsteps.

Dad showed me a bunk I could use.

"What do we do next?" I asked.

"We go to sleep. The train we'll take back to Staples will be here in a couple of hours."

A cool breeze blew through the screen door as I snuggled under the covers. I was still smiling when I closed my eyes and slipped into a quiet, restful sleep. I dreamt of being the engineer on my own diesel locomotive. It was gigantic, powerful and gleamed in the sun! I was just about to start climbing the ladder to board my new silver engine when I felt something pulling on my boot. "Time to wake up, Kenny, we have another train to catch."

It was still dark when the taxi dropped us off at the "yards" in Dilworth. I don't know how he did it, but Dad had gotten us some breakfast. It wasn't much--a couple donuts, a cup of coffee for him and a cup of orange juice for me. But on that morning, breakfast had never tasted so good.

This time, as the train roared down the tracks toward home, through sleepy slits, I located the water cooler and got my own cup of ice cold water.

I knew the rising sun was casting long shadows across the railroad yards when the train came to a stop near the Staples depot. Dad got down from the engine first, and then helped me off that last step.

Walking across the tracks to our waiting car, blue and white striped engineer's cap on my head and grip in my hand, I imagined my shadow falling against the rocks, rails and ties. It was a tall shadow. Tall, like I felt, 'cause my dad and I had been workin' on the railroad!

"Kenny, what's that on your arm?" Mom was curious.

"Nothing, Mom, just mosquito bites."

"Can I have a look at them?"

"Sure."

She took one look at my arm and called the doctor. It was poison ivy—again. Poison Ivy was becoming a summer tradition.

My itching arms puffed up like Popeyes'. I'd lie on the floor and listen to cartoons with a towel under each arm to collect the unwanted ooze. After the towels were soaked, Mom would bring in two more and my arms just continued oozing.

Mom and Dad tried to figure out how I got it.

"Could he have sensitive skin?" Mom wondered. "Some people can get it, just from the wind."

"Doubtful," he responded. "He must pick it up when he is out playing. But where?"

Dad kept our lawn plush and green as a golf course. He knew there was no poison ivy there. Another possibility was my great-uncle Ken's place, just a few blocks away from ours. But Ken's love for his yard and flower beds ensured there would be no poison ivy there, either.

After my arms had returned to their normal size, Dad asked me where else I played besides our neighborhood and Ken's place.

"Sometimes I ride my bike to the sand pits or the playground."

Dad knew both of those areas and neither had poison ivy.

"Is there anywhere else?"

"No, not really," I said. "Oh, yeah, there is my fort..."

My fort was located on the far side of the vacant lot behind our house. Made from an old cardboard box, it was right next to the ditch that ran along Fourth Street. At one time it may have held a stove or something like that, but now it was my hiding place

"Could you show us your fort?" Dad asked.

"Sure, it's really cool back there."

When we pushed our way past the last bit of tall grass and I proudly gestured towards my fort, my folks were speechless. I thought it was because they were impressed by my terrific fort, but that is not what caught their attention. They were looking past my fort at the ditch. Its bottom and sides were thickly lined with reddish, three leafed plants.

It sounded like a bunch of the neighborhood kids were in the back lot behind our house. Their voices were joyful and enthusiastic. They were saying things like: "Let's go, team!" and "we can win this one easy!" Curious, I went to see what was going on.

"Hey, Kenny, we need one more player on our team. Come and join us." It was Dale, one of the older boys who lived across the street from us.

"Okay," I hesitated, "where should I go?"

"Our side is up to bat. Just stay here with us. You bat after David."

I felt a bit apprehensive about playing. The only thing I had ever done with a ball and bat was to toss the ball up in the air and then try to hit it, missing most of the time. Nevertheless, they needed me and I figured a poor player must be better than no player at all.

One by one my teammates went to bat. With two on base and two outs, David hit a home run, making it my turn to bat.

My insides felt like it was time to take a test at school. The buzz of the field insects sounded like a freight train and the sun seemed just a little hotter than usual. With clammy hands, I picked up a bat and took my place by the crude board we called home plate.

Looking out to the field in the direction of our make-shift pitcher's mound, I squinted and strained to pick up any movement. Then "thud" and "ste-e-rike one!" I stood there amazed. I had no idea that the ball had even been pitched.

"Okay, wait a minute!" Dale was stopping the game! "We need to make some adjustments. Kenny isn't seeing the ball. How about if the pitcher moves half way between his mound and home plate? Let's try that."

Everyone agreed it was a fair move and once again I took my position. This time when the ball was pitched, one of my team mates yelled, "Here it comes!" While straining to see any movement in the haze ahead of me, once again I heard "thud" and "ste-e-rike two!"

"Hold it, wait a minute." Dale interrupted the game again. "Let's try rolling the ball on the ground."

The next time the ball was pitched, bumping its way across the uneven ground, I could tell where it was. Swinging the bat at the bouncing crunch, I hit it, or perhaps "golfed" it would be more accurate. Not knowing exactly where first base was, I took off in its general direction.

"Over here, Kenny!" Following the sound of his voice, I heard the "thud" in his mitt. And the inning was over. It was time to switch sides. Now someone else could bat.

While their intentions were good, I didn't like being treated "special." It bothered me that the pitcher had to move in close and roll me the ball. I wanted to be treated just like the others.

Dale assigned me to right field. That was fine with me. I wanted to be away from the action, far away.

Each time I heard the "crack" of the bat my stomach would tense and I would pray that it would not come in my direction. It could go anywhere, as long as it was far away from me. If it were to come my way I wasn't sure I could catch it, or find it if it hit the ground and rolled.

Then I heard it, the "crack" followed by someone yelling, "Kenny, it's a high fly ball headin' in your direction!"

I scanned the empty sky for movement. Nothing. Then the dull "thump," two smaller "bumps" and the crackle of dry field grass as the ball rolled to a stop. The crackling ball was easy to follow until it stopped making noise.

"To your left! It's to your left!" someone yelled.

Moving two or three steps to my left, I looked down, searching the formless gray at my feet for a light colored circle. Nothing caught my attention.

"Right in front of you! It's right in front of you!"

By this time everyone was yelling directions. I knew that if I didn't hurry, the runner would make it to home plate and score. My teammates were counting on me to stop him and I couldn't even see where the ball was. Everything in front of me was smeared together, no detail, no ball. A lump formed in my throat.

"Two feet in front of your left shoe!"

Dropping to my hands and knees, I searched the grass in front of me. There it was! I grabbed it, jumped to my feet and threw it as hard as I could in the direction of home plate. I missed it by a mile. My poor throw didn't make any difference anyway. The runner had scored before I had even found the ball.

When the game was over I felt incredibly angry and very much alone. I hated the fact that I had to be treated different than the others. I didn't want to be different. I wanted to play baseball like everyone else.

Nobody made fun of me that day. No one said: "Hey, batter, you blind or what?" No one ridiculed my lousy throw to home, or my inability to find first base. But when the game was over and everyone had gone home, I was still alone and feeling trapped in my world of blurs and smudges.

That afternoon Mom walked into our living room to find me sitting on the floor in front of the TV listening to Oral Roberts. My hand was reaching up to touch the TV screen, my head bowed in prayer. He was asking God for a miracle. He was asking God to heal all those who had placed their hands on their TV screens. He was asking God to heal them of all their sicknesses and diseases.

She left the room as her own vision began to blur.

Chapter 4

———————

Nose in the Books

The zing of the table saw stopped and I pulled my fingers out of my ears. The smell of cedar and fresh cut pine made me smile. Great uncle Ken and I were in his basement workshop making a wooden boat that we were going to launch from the small bridge over the creek behind his house. When he wasn't working on the railroad, Ken was downstairs working on one of his many projects. When I'd go to visit, he always had a hammer, nails and chunk of wood for me so I could work on one of my many projects, too.

The ringing phone upstairs was followed by Grandma's footsteps to the basement door. "Kenny, your mom just called. Your case worker arrived and she wants to see you."

Leaving their house using the outside basement steps, I jumped on my bike and headed for home.

Mom returned to the living room. "He'll be just a minute, he was visiting his grandma. She only lives a couple blocks away and..." Looking out the window she could see me coming down the street. "Here he comes now."

Our case worker looked out the window. "Where is he?"

"Right down the street."

Once again our case worker looked out the window searching the sidewalks for me. Seeing no one, she turned to Mom.

"Where? I don't see him."

"In the red shirt, almost at the intersection."

"I'm sorry, but I still don't..."

Zipping up the driveway, I slammed on the brakes and headed for the door.

Once inside, I learned the reason for her visit. She had brought me a reel-to-reel tape recorder to help in my school work. Many of my text books were on tape and that machine would let me listen to them. Included with the recorder was a microphone, a set of headphones, a wire she said I "shouldn't mess with," a blank tape and the take-up reel. Each was in its own plastic bag.

Each bag we opened smelled like a new toy. The bag with the wire that I "wasn't supposed to mess with" was left alone. She took a few minutes to show me where to plug in the mike and headphones and how to pull the tape from the full reel, past the heads, between the capstan and pinch roller and finally, onto the take up reel.

The controls were smooth to the touch and easy to operate. Each one was shaped differently than the others and I memorized their functions quickly.

The recorder fit nicely on my desk next to my "talking book" machine. On that machine I listened to "talking books" that came in big black cartons from the Library of Congress. Tom Sawyer and Huck Finn were my good buddies on the Mississippi and I could feel the cold in *Call of the Wild.*

Having completed her delivery of the recorder and a brief training session in its operation, our case worker closed her briefcase and walked to the door.

"I think Kenny has a bright future ahead of him. He can do anything he puts his mind to."

Mom took a deep breath before she spoke. "Well, we haven't really taught him that he can do anything he wants to." She emphasized the word *anything.* "Right now he wants to be a railroad engineer like his father."

It didn't take me long to realize that the recorder could do more than just play-back my homework. I discovered that if I set the little square microphone in front of our small transistor radio and turned the recorder to *record*, I could tape the music that was playing on WCCO. Sadly, when I played the tape back it never sounded as good as the original. It always seemed to pick up other noises, like cars driving by outside or Cinder yipping at something in the front yard.

Flawed as those recordings were, I loved every minute of my young recording career. Taping songs off the radio was something I could do; it was a source of success. The tapes gave me something to feel proud of. Unlike baseball, success with a tape recorder did not depend on my vision.

It was really starting to bug me. Every time I'd reach into that compartment to get the mike, I'd bump that bag with the wire that I wasn't supposed to "mess with." Each time I'd touch it, I'd wonder what it could be for. Finally, my curiosity got the best of me.

One night after supper while I was supposed to be listening to a book, I pulled that bag out of its compartment and opened it. Enjoying the new toy smell, I examined the cable inside. One end had a plug, like the one on the mike. The other end had two small clips on it. They reminded me of tiny alligator jaws, complete with sharp little teeth. They were ready to clip to something, —but what?

I remembered replacing the batteries in our transistor radio in the kitchen a couple days earlier. Unsnapping the back of the radio had revealed the battery compartment, the chassis and the speaker. Two wires ran from the chassis to each side of the speaker. They connected to two little tabs, one on the left and one on the right. Two clips on the wire, two tabs on the speaker. I wondered if...

Dad was at work and Mom was in the back yard talking to June, our neighbor. I turned up the volume on my "talking book" machine so it sounded like I was reading. Side six of *Treasure Island* would cover up any noise I might make on my way down the hall.

I listened at my bedroom door to see if all was quiet in the house. Then I scampered down the hall to get the transistor radio and tip-toed back to my room. All was quiet except for Long John Silver in my bedroom. So far, so good.

Unsnapping the back of the radio, I explored its contents. There they were, just as I had remembered. Two tabs on the speaker— just the right size for those little alligator jaws. I put the blank tape on the recorder, hooked the clips to the speaker and plugged the other end of the cable into the mike jack.

Taking a deep breath, I started the recorder. I ran my tongue over my lips one more time, said a quick prayer and turned on the radio. Nothing exploded— and I could hear WCCO loud and clear. But was it being recorded? I plugged in the headphones and there it was. WCCO, crisp and clean. I let the song play a bit longer and then rewound the tape. With trembling fingers, I pushed "play" and there it was. "Tammy's in Love" never sounded so good.

The entire classroom was quiet as we labored over our math quiz. My teacher had provided me with a copy she had made that had numbers that were two inches high. Hunched over my desk, chewing on my pencil, I was trying to remember how to multiply a one digit number by a two digit number when I felt a tap on my shoulder. It was Mrs. Johnson, the school secretary.

She spoke softly. "When you finish the quiz, would you come down to the principal's office?"

"Umm, sure—okay." I whispered.

An icy chill ran down my spine. I had heard stories about students who were called to the principal's office. Some were never seen again. Why was I being asked to go there? What had I done?

Maybe it had to do with yesterday. I had to stay after school because I was talking during our social studies lesson. Staying after wouldn't have been so bad except I had my Cub Scout meeting right after school and I was wearing my uniform. Having to stay after the bell was embarrassing. Cub Scouts were supposed to set a good example and there I was standing in the corner facing the wall.

Arriving at the principal's office, I learned that my visit was not about my talking during class. The school had received my new large print math book. Mrs. Johnson wanted me to look it over to see if it would work for me.

The book on the table in front of me had been ordered directly from the publisher. Brand new, it was made up of six volumes. Each volume was approximately an inch and a half thick, twenty four inches tall and about sixteen inches wide. The books still had the thin plastic covering over them. Peeling back the plastic allowed the thick smell of glue and ink to fill the room.

As I opened the first book, its binding crackled like Rice Krispies. The contents and layout of each page were identical to that of my small print math book, except that the print and diagrams were much larger. The page numbers in my large print book corresponded exactly to those in my small print edition.

Mrs. Johnson said that I should take only the volume we were using in class and leave the others in her office. Heavier than a guilty conscience, I carried the monster back to my classroom and plopped it on my desk. When it was open, it covered the whole desk top, leaving me no room to write.

Yet even with the help of the large print I still couldn't read the text without additional magnification so we looked around for a suitable magnifying glass. All that we could find was the "Sherlock Holmes" type with the handle and the rounded glass. None of them had enough power.

On our next routine visit to the Mayo clinic, we found a magnifier that did have the right amount of power. Originally designed as a paper weight, it was about three inches in diameter and two inches thick at its center. Dome shaped on one side, flat on the other, it fit very nicely in the right front pocket of my corduroy pants.

Writing presented its own set of difficulties. In very early grades as we learned how to write, the penmanship paper was fairly easy to use. Each page had thick dark lines on it, plus a line in the middle, to help us as we formed our letters. If I got very close to the paper and used dull point, soft lead pencils, I could see the character I was writing.

In higher grades my teachers said that I could continue to use the "penmanship paper" if I wanted to. But after I got my magnifier, I found I could hold it off the paper at an angle and see through it as I wrote. That method allowed me to use standard theme paper like the other kids.

All of the students in the fifth grade were expected to be in the flute-a-phone band and I was no exception. Made from plastic, it was about a foot long and smelled brand new. My fingers fit over the holes on the front perfectly and my thumbs curved around back to support the instrument. The mouth piece was smooth and ready for my first toot.

The only obstacle between me and my successful flute-a-phone career was the music. It was too small—much too small. Holding my magnifier on the music and trying to play my instrument at the same time just didn't work.

The answer to this dilemma came through Mrs. Johnson. She was kind enough to make copies of my music with large notes—by hand using black markers and sheets of typing paper. Turned sideways, she could fit four to six measures on a page. Each note was between three and four inches tall.

At first, our band worked on scales but quickly progressed to "Mary had a little lamb." Tempos were slow and it was easy to stop and turn pages. Reading the notes was easy if I kept my nose about five inches from the music. I wanted to learn how to play because next year I could be in the marching band and that meant the parade.

Every Fourth of July our family went to watch the parade. Standing on the curb listening to the parade go by was a mix of highs and lows. The floats were boring. I couldn't see what they were supposed to be and they rarely made noise or played music. Sometimes people around me would make comments to each other like, "Wow, look at that." Looking toward the road to see what they were talking about, all I'd see was a shapeless blob moving slowly down the street. All I could hear was the sound of the streamers flapping in the wind or swishing against the pavement. Very uninspiring.

Oh, but when the band came by, my whole world trembled from my ears down to my tennis shoes!

Quiet at first, barely heard above the rustle of leaves in the trees, I could hear the band coming when it was still far away. First was the crisp snap of the snare drums, then the deep steady beat of the bass. Then the brass instruments joined in, louder and louder still. Soon the band was right in front of us.

When the trumpets let loose on "Stars and Stripes Forever," my imagination went wild. I could see myself, proudly wearing the uniform of the Staples High School Band, all of us marching in perfect harmony to the beat of the big bass drum, our heads held high. What an honor.

Choosing an instrument for sixth grade band was pretty easy. Since I needed to get close to the music, the saxophone was the logical choice. With a sax I could get closer to the music than a trumpet or trombone.

As time went on, my skill level increased and the music moved from note to note much more quickly than before. More time was being spent turning pages than tooting my horn.

Making the pages bigger was impractical. They could be the same size, but the notes had to be smaller. If the notes were smaller, my nose would have to be closer to the music. With my sax, I couldn't get any closer.

We asked my band teacher, Mr. Evans, if he had any suggestions.

"How about switching from sax to flute? The fingering positions are nearly the same so you wouldn't have to learn a new instrument from scratch. The flute would allow you to get real close to the music."

Staying in the band was important because summer was coming and it would be time to play "Stars and Stripes Forever."

Following the flute part was next to impossible. It must have had a billion notes and they were all played super fast. I couldn't move my head across the page fast enough to keep up with the tempo. The only thing left to do was to memorize it.

Mom and I spent many hours going over the song again and again and again. I could feel my enthusiasm for band disappearing, and it was disappearing very fast. The joy of being in band was being overshadowed by my frustration at having to work so hard to learn the music.

When the day of the Fourth of July parade arrived, I put on my uniform and Mom dropped me off at the depot where the other band members were already forming the lines for the march. Some band members were warming up their instruments, creating a musical din and others were just waiting for the parade to begin. Finding my place in line, I blew a couple notes to warm up. Then the drum major blew his whistle and everyone was quiet and stood at attention. The drums set the cadence and away we went, past the fire station and left at city hall. Continuing down Fourth Street to the cemetery, the parade concluded with ceremonies and a short program.

Weighing the fun of marching in the band and the long hours of memorization, I decided it might be best to learn to play the guitar.

Mid-winter sun flooded through large windows on the west side of the library making the tables bright and warm.

Piling my books on one of the tables and pulling my magnifying glass from my pocket, I sat down and opened my science book, ready to study. Setting the magnifying glass on the page, I leaned over the table and looked through the glass.

I had only read a few words when I felt a firm hand against the back of my head. The hand was pushing down. It was pushing my face into the book. In response, the muscles in my neck tightened in an effort to push back, but the unseen hand was too strong. My nose was being crunched onto the page and my cheek was sliding across the oval glass of my magnifier. Then as quickly as it had come, the pushing hand was gone.

Stunned, I turned around in hopes of seeing someone. The library seemed empty. No one had made fun of my blindness before. I had never been the brunt of a cruel joke, nor had I been mocked because of my lack of sight. Not until that brief moment.

Physically, I had not been hurt. My nose was unharmed and my cheek had only bumped against my magnifier. Nevertheless, in that moment, the unseen hand had left a message.

The message was loud and clear: "Ken, you look pretty stupid sitting there hunched over that book. Real stupid! What's wrong with you anyway?"

In my adolescent darkroom, I was developing a picture of myself. In that instant, the picture, as I gazed into the tray of chemicals, was flawed. It was different. It was unacceptable.

Sitting up straight in my chair, I put my magnifier back in my pocket and closed the book. My brain told me it was no big deal. "Get used to it, that sort of thing will happen all your life. Just ignore it."

Taking the message that had been sent, combining it with the unacceptable picture in the darkroom tray, I made a decision. "Okay," I reasoned, "I don't like to be different and I don't like to look stupid. I am different because of my blindness and look stupid when I read. Therefore—I'll never read in public again! Then I'll be accepted. Then I'll be like the others. No one has to know that I can't see."

Satisfied with my decision, I walked to the magazine rack and removed the latest issue of LOOK. Sitting down in the nearest easy chair, with the magazine open in my lap, I pretended to read until the bell rang announcing the end of the school day.

Chapter 5

———————

Alphabetical Order is Good!

Mrs. Bushee stood in front of our ninth grade English class to make a special announcement.

"Before we begin our lesson today I want to let you all know that the junior high English classes will be joining together to present the one-act play 'Tom Sawyer's Morning.' Several acting parts are available and we need some stage hands as well.

Try-outs will be held here this evening at seven o'clock. I hope to have the cast chosen by the end of the week and will post that list on the bulletin board outside this classroom. Rehearsals will begin next week and will be held each evening at seven."

Concentrating on the lesson that day was impossible. My mind was playing around with the idea of trying out for a part. Being in a play wouldn't be like sports, where you had to watch a ball, or like band that involved following tiny notes up and down the musical staff. Acting was something I thought I could do, something I could do with the other students.

Being part of the cast would mean we were all on common ground. No one needed to be treated special or work extra hard to keep up. We all would have to memorize our own parts; we all would have to learn where to walk and where to stand on stage. All of us would have to learn how to "act", and learning to act was something I knew I could do. My vision wouldn't even be an issue.

Returning to school that evening I could hear voices echoing down the hall on my way to Mrs. Bushee's room. The regular seating arrangement had been changed. Desks were now lined up along the walls leaving an open space in the center.

"Hey, Ken, there's an empty chair over here!" It was my good friend Steve Adams. I quickly sat down.

"Wow, lots of kids! Who all is here?" What I really wanted to know was how fierce the competition for parts was going to be.

"The room is full, I don't know everyone. From our grade I see Mark Schultenover and David Uhrich, from eighth grade there's Brian Wise, Guy Doud and Steve Eskelson. There are even a couple girls from our grade, Karen Marden and Kathy Simkins."

Mrs. Bushee walked to the middle of the room. "I want to thank everyone for coming. Before we begin, I'd like to give you a brief overview of the play." She cleared her throat. "It takes place in Tom's front yard on a Saturday morning. He skipped school on Friday so his Aunt Polly is punishing him by making him stay home and paint the fence. As the play unfolds, we find various characters walking past his house and Tom tries to trick them into doing his painting for him. Okay, that's the play in brief, let's start reading. Everyone turn to the top of page 158. Brian, you read Tom's lines and David, you read Huckelberry's lines." She sat down and the try outs began.

Listening to my classmates read their assigned parts, my heart sank. They all read their lines smoothly and some even added expression.

Reading aloud was part of trying out. I hated the thought of getting up in front of everyone and stumbling through my lines while juggling my magnifier and script on the end of my nose. If, however, reading in public again meant a part in the play, I'd give it a try.

"Ken," My face flushed. "You read Huckleberry and Steve, you read Tom."

Standing to my feet, I took a few steps foreword into the open part of the room.

"Huckleberry, you start."

Peering through my magnifier, I found my lines and started reading. I could only see about three words at a time. And, to make matters worse, my lines were mixed with stage instructions. The reading was jerky and painfully slow. I even got lost a couple of times. Then after what seemed like a lifetime, she interrupted us and called on two other students. Sitting down, I knew I had done a lousy job.

Two days later I was walking down the hall to my locker when I heard someone running up behind me. It was Steve.

"Ken, she's putting up the cast list; let's go check it out."

Walking quickly down the hall, I was not as enthusiastic as Steve. I had resigned myself to being a stage hand.

Standing in front of the bulletin board, Steve searched the list for our names.

"Mmm...let's see. Hey, I'm Huckleberry Finn." He continued reading the list. "Mark plays Jim...and you...oh man, you're Tom Sawyer."

An almost permanent grin stretched across my face as I tried to take in the news.

"Who else got parts?"

"David, Karen, Brian, Guy, Mark, Steve and Kathy." He paused a long time before he spoke again. This time his voice had lost its smile.

"Kathy is going to be Becky Thatcher."

"So?"

"I think the script says..." His voice trailed off for a moment.

"Says what?"

"I think you're in big trouble man. I read the last part of the script when I was waiting for try outs to start and, well..."

"Well, what?" I was getting impatient.

"The script says Tom has to kiss Becky."

"What? Kiss a girl! No way!"

"I'm afraid so."

"You lie like a rug. Let's go look it up."

We practically flew into Mrs. Bushee's room to pick up our scripts. Steve scanned the text and found the offending passage. There it was on the top of page 165, inside the parenthesis, in italics the stage directions read: "Finding no one in sight, he quickly gives Becky a slight peck on the cheek."

"Well, it's not really a kiss." I sputtered. "It's a 'peck'...on the cheek. No big deal."

Further examination of the script revealed that Tom had been talking about love, kissing and engagement since page 162.

"Good grief, what am I gonna do?"

"It's just a play, don't worry about it."

"That's easy for you to say. You're Huckleberry Finn. You don't have to kiss a girl."

Crossing the gym on my way to choir, I heard it. The music became louder and clearer and I started to hum the happy melody. Irene was at the piano and "Seventy Six Trombones" was echoing down the hallway. Mr. Carlson had chosen "The Music Man" as our tenth grade musical. We rehearsed the songs every day in choir and worked on the acting, staging and choreography after school.

I was cast as Tommy Djilas, the young prankster who nearly gives the mayor's wife a heart attack when he sets off firecrackers at the Fourth of July celebration. Tommy also has an interest in the mayor's daughter, Zaneeta Schinn. Guess who was cast in that role. That's right, Becky Thatcher.

Learning my lines was not difficult and the music was fun to sing. However, musicals are more than just dialog and songs. They are also filled with dancing. That's the part that really drove me crazy: the dance number that takes place in the library. In this scene the music man, Harold Hill, visits the library to try and sweet talk Marian, the librarian, into a date. His pleas turn into song and soon everyone in the library is dancing around the tables and chairs—including Tommy and Zaneeta.

The dance steps were easy to learn. I did, however, have difficulty with one of the movements.

At one point, the ladies are atop the library tables twirling and swishing their colorful costumes. In the middle of the song, in one effortless movement, all the guys would gently take their partners by the waist and carry them gracefully through the air and set them softly on the floor where they continued the dance.

Weighing just less than ninety pounds, my ability to give Zaneeta a smooth ride from table top to floor was in serious doubt. While the other older and bigger guys were allowing their partners to float gracefully from table to floor, I felt fortunate to keep Zaneeta from breaking her ankle. Every night after practice when she got home, Kathy would slam the door behind her and vehemently announce to her mother, "I do not like that Ken Miller! Why do they keep casting us together?"

Days and evenings at Staples High were filled with classes, club meetings and after school activities. If I wasn't working on a project for Science Club, rehearsing a play for Drama Club or editing page two for the Kardinal Kronicle, I was with Steve learning new music for our rock band.

Weekends were spent going to movies, sporting events and the Lucky Leprechaun Cafe with my friends. Late Friday and Saturday nights I'd put on my headphones and see what was on the shortwave radio that had been loaned to me by a local ham radio operator.

Yet amid all the fun, friends, and activities there was one area of my life that I refused to acknowledge. One subject that was much more than what I could deal with--my future. Like a child who eats the hot dog and chips first, hoping the peas on his plate will magically disappear, I enjoyed my present and ignored my future, hoping it, like the peas, would disappear.

If I dared to stop my activity long enough to think about it, I knew I'd be haunted by insecurity and gripped by fear. After all, what kind of work is a blind man going to find? What will I do? Where will I go? Who would hire me? What is going to happen to me? What will my life look like in twenty years?

Each time I tapped into that area of my life I was overwhelmed by the specter of an unknown and uncertain future. It was too much to deal with so I kept it at arm's length like a quarterback fending off the opposition. I didn't like the way it felt when I thought about it, so I didn't think about it.

I wasn't the only person wrestling with the future. Our whole nation seemed to be groaning under a burden far heavier than it could bear.

Since early elementary school we had been having Civil Defense drills and everyone knew how to get to the fall-out shelter. The Cuban missile crisis had come and gone. We sat in our classrooms and listened in utter disbelief as our teachers told us that school was going to be let out early because our president had been shot.

Books like Animal Farm and 1984 were required reading in our English classes. Our nation was in the midst of a conflict in Southeast Asia that no one understood. Back home, peaceful protests were turning violent and tempers were being lost. Musicians raised their voices to be heard at public gatherings and over the air waves. At the march on Washington, Peter, Paul and Mary were wishing for a hammer while the radio broadcast Barry McGuire's musical question: "Don't you know we're on the eve of destruction."

Despite personal worries and future fears, plans for post-high school education still needed to be made. Many of my classmates were going to attend St. Cloud State and others, like Jim Durbin and Kathy Simkins, had chosen Moorhead State. It seemed logical, since Dad was in Moorhead quite often bringing trains to and from Staples, that Moorhead would be a good choice for me, particularly when I ran out of pizza money.

During my senior year, I related to the same group of kids that I knew from choir, drama club and church. We didn't do much dating, as in "couples," but when the weekend came we always had something going on.

Of course there were those times when we did date as couples, like Homecoming and the Christmas dance. On those occasions Steve and I would double-date in his brown '56 Pontiac. I enjoyed those dates, but none of the girls captured my attention until the New Year's Eve party at my place in 1969.

The evening was filled with music, munching, Twister and ping pong. Mine wasn't the only party going on that New Year's Eve and it seemed like people were coming or going all night long.

Moments before midnight I heard footsteps coming down the stairs. More guests were arriving. Standing at the bottom of the steps, I welcomed the newcomers. Duane, Jim, Cindy and Kathy made it just in time to hear the count down to 1970. As Kathy breezed past, she gave me a peck on the cheek and proclaimed "Happy New Year!" Then she was gone into the crowd.

Unaccustomed to such a lavish show of affection my mind started to play games with my heart.

"Why did she do that? Is she interested in me?"

"No, kissing is customary on New Year's Eve."

"Oh, but what if she likes me?"

"Don't even think about it. Put it out of your mind."

We were part of the same group of kids who hung out together. My heart was distracted anytime she was around. Trying to put it out of my mind would be like telling a tree to fly south for the winter. It just wasn't gonna happen.

Observing her pleasant disposition, the way she related to others, her zest for life, her kind heart and that great perfume she always wore made me want to be around her as much as possible.

But beyond my feelings for her, two important questions remained: First, how does she feel about me? And second, how can I find out?

Reading her non-verbal communication was out of the question. She could pass me in the hall at Staples High with a big sign that said: "Ken Miller, ask me out on a date. Please!" and I wouldn't even see it. Then there was the direct approach: just walk up to her and ask. Nope, too much risk. It would be totally humiliating if she responded to my question with the seven dreaded words that every teenager struck by Cupid's arrow fears the most, "I like you as a friend, but..."

So, after eliminating non-verbal and spoken indicators, only one possibility remained: vibes. Vibes are those mysterious things that can be sensed between two people. I'd been told it happens in movies and on TV something like this: He looks across the crowded room to see his soon-to-be girlfriend, their eyes meet and boom, they feel the vibes. No eyes meeting in this case, but maybe a vibe or two would do.

The best spot to meet her and check for vibes was her locker. She had to go there before school and after school. And I had a good excuse to be there because my friend Mark Schultenover had his locker right next to Kathy Simkins. I could be at his locker and know that I would see her at least once a day. Alphabetical order is good!

Valentine's Day was getting close and I still couldn't think of a gift for Kathy. I knew of two other guys that were getting her something, so my gift had to be unique. It had to be something that would stand out in a crowd. Perfume? No, if I gave her some, she might feel like she had to wear it and I liked the stuff she had. How 'bout the latest Beatles record? Nope, she may have it already. How about flowers? Williams Nursery was on the other end of town—too far to walk. How about candy? No again, too generic.

The answer to my dilemma came a few days later. That morning when she opened her locker the bottle of Corn Huskers hand lotion she used every day after art class fell to the floor. It shattered into a million pieces at my feet. It was the perfect gift. After all, nothing says: "Be My Valentine" like a bottle of Corn Huskers!

Skaife Drug was a short walk from school and after Mr. Longbella helped me locate the lotion, I was ready for the next part of my plan: getting the combination to Kathy's locker.

Always up for a little fun, Mark took a peek at the spinning numbers the next time she visited her locker. He wrote the combination in giant letters on a piece of notebook paper and gave it to me between classes. So far, so good.

I stayed after school extra late that day to be sure she had gone home. Counting lockers from the nearest classroom door, I found Kathy's and pulled my most powerful magnifying glass from my pocket. I wanted to be sure to open the combination lock on the first try. One good squint and two twists of the wrist later and her locker was open. Placing the lotion on the top shelf, I closed the door and listened to see if I'd been seen. All was quiet.

The next day, in order to get to school before Kathy, I left the Frosted Flakes in the cupboard and rushed out the door fifteen minutes earlier than usual. I felt like a little kid on Christmas Eve. My bike tires didn't touch the ground on the whole ride to school. Mark was already at his locker so we pretended to talk about an English assignment when she arrived.

"Hi, guys." She set her books on top of her locker.

"Good morning, Kathy," we said in unison.

Eyeing us suspiciously, she turned the combination on her lock and opened the door.

"What is this?"

"What is what?" We tried to sound innocent.

She reached to the shelf and picked up the bottle of lotion and the card taped to it. The card said simply, "Be My Valentine."

"Well, thank you. Thank you very much. I love it!"

I wasn't sure, but was that a vibe in her voice? I think it was. Oh yes, alphabetical order is good!

The early spring air was chilly as we climbed aboard our bus for the return trip. Our high school choir had traveled to Long Prairie to see their school present the musical Oklahoma! While it's true I enjoyed the musical, the best part of the evening was sitting next to Kathy on the bus.

We didn't talk much during the trip home. It was enough for us just to be together. Finding one another, our hands seemed to join our hearts in a silent game of affectionate communication. Each time I gave her hand a gentle squeeze, she responded with a squeeze of her own. Even though the squeezes were undefined, I jumped for joy every time one was returned. The game lasted the entire trip back to Staples.

As we left the bus I could hear Duane's voice.

"Hey, Kathy and Ken-want a ride home?" Not many of our classmates had cars, but Duane was one of them and we gladly accepted.

The front seat was already full so we jumped in the back. We sat close to one another, partly to keep the cold away, partly because I didn't want the evening to end.

Once again my hand found hers. Unbelief flooded my heart and mind every time she returned a squeeze. This can't be happening to me, I thought. But it was true. No one was making her do it, but there it was-another squeeze. No strings were attached, yet, there she was.

50

I had never felt that way about another person before. Being with Kathy was special, not like being with the guys or even other girls. She had the power to make me a king in my own court, or make me a fool on the floor.

The radio was tuned to WLS. Chicago and the Temptations were singing, ".....What can make me feel this way? My girl...." Squeezing her hand once again, I knew exactly what they meant.

Until that moment our relationship had been light and fun, but sitting next to her, holding her hand, I realized that my feelings for her were more than playful friendship. In fact, did I see a wedding in the future? Did I see a happily-ever-after? Kids? A house? A dog in the yard? I couldn't wait a moment longer. I had to break the silence. I had to tell her how I felt. It was now, or never!

Letting go of her hand and putting my arm around her, I whispered in her ear.

"Kathy, I love you."

Her soft cheek brushed mine as she leaned to my ear, her breath tickled as she whispered, "Are you sure it's not just infatuation?"

Hey, not fair! She just shoved me off the back of a speeding pick up truck and left me in the dust! Where did that come from?

Wiping the ice water from my face and flicking the cubes from my collar, I realized the source could only be found in one place, her church. She was Lutheran, while I was Methodist. If this relationship was going to go very far, she'd have to convert. You'd never catch a Methodist using that kind of language.

Chapter 6

Batman on a Bike

Summer time after my senior year had arrived and the livin' was easy. Kathy worked at the Dairy Dip, a short bike ride from my place; I worked part time in the print shop at the vocational school.

One afternoon a commercial on KWAD radio caught my attention. It advertised a Beatle's double feature at the Rand Drive-in near Verndale. "A Hard Day's Night" was set to start at dusk, followed by "Help". I wanted to take Kathy, but was not sure how to work out the transportation details. During the school year we either hitched rides with friends or went on double dates. But with school out and everyone on different schedules, it was not as easy to get around.

My parents had offered us their car when we wanted to go out. That meant, of course, the ol' Ford station wagon, not the snappy '67 Mustang convertible. They even offered to drive me over to Kathy's house to pick her up. I liked the idea of using their car, but was not crazy about the idea of being chauffeured on our date—even if it was just a short ride across town. After all, I did have my eighteen-year-old ego to protect.

Giving the matter some serious thought, I came up with a plan that seemed workable: I'd ride my bike to her house, pick her up and give her a ride back to my place. From there we'd take the car to the movie. After the movie, we'd drive back to Staples and I'd bring her home on my trusty three-speed Huffy.

Knowing Kathy would enjoy the movies, I called and told her about my plan. "Since my bike is not a bicycle built for two," I explained, "You will have to ride side saddle on the bar that runs between the seat and the handlebars." Good sport that she is, she gave skeptical agreement to my plan.

To make her ride as smooth as possible, I took the three-by-six-foot pink shag rug from the back of our station wagon, folded it a few times and laid it over the bar.

Arriving a bit after seven, she was already waiting for me by the edge of the road outside her house holding a sweater.

"What's the sweater for? It's hot out."

"For the ride home. It's gonna be chilly by the time we get back."

Then she paused before speaking again. "Are you sure this is going to work?"

"Yup."

I kept my left foot on the pedal and my right foot on the curb for balance. "All you do is stand on the curb with your back to me, take hold of the handlebars and lean back onto the rug. I'll do the rest."

"Okay, if you say so." She grabbed the handle bars and leaned back, I gave the bike an extra hard pump and we were on our way to the movies!

Turning onto Wisconsin Avenue, I watched the large house and tree shapes to my left. When they were gone, I knew I was passing an open field and getting close to the shortcut through the railroad yards. The shortcut was a sandy path that ran through a grassy field and then past the "round house." Its pale shading, contrasted with the darker shading of the grass, made it easy to identify and follow. Next, the path became a board walk that crossed the tracks and led to the depot and onto Fourth Street.

When we arrived at the curb in front of my house, Kathy executed a graceful dismount from the bike. Our trip was accident free. We didn't even have a close call. The keys were in the car and soon we were on the road to the drive-in.

We parked in the second row and I used my monocular to view the screen. This was the first time I had used it at a drive-in and I found it frustrating because I had to keep moving it to follow the action. It seemed that every time I'd watch the right side of the screen, the action was on the left and if I watched the left side, the action was on the right. When I'd get lost trying to follow the antics of the "Fab Four", I could always find temporary relief in our bucket of hot-buttered popcorn.

It was near two o'clock in the morning before we entered the Staples' city limits. The eighty degree day had turned into a sixty-degree evening. Off in the distance I could hear a whistle blow as a freight train rolled through town.

My bike was in the garage where I'd left it, rug in place, ready to go. Kathy put on her sweater and waited at the curb as I got the bike in position. One hard pedal and we were on our way.

We snuggled close, which was easy to do, to keep the cool away on the ride across town. Street lights helped guide me down Fourth Street. The only sound was the occasional crunch of sand or gravel under my tires and the crickets along the road. It seemed the town was asleep.

Passing the depot, we left the street lights behind and found the railroad yards bathed in moon light. Sweet clover filled the air as we rolled onto the board walk.

Kathy's hair tickled my nose as she turned to face me. "I need to tell you something."

"What?"

"Lean closer," she whispered.

"What?" I leaned closer to hear.

"I love you."

My front tire went off the left side of the board walk tossing us both from the bike. Kathy simply stood as the bike fell. I untangled myself from the fallen bike, knocked the cinders from my palms and wondered if anyone could be any happier than I was at that very moment. "She loves me, yeah, yeah, yeah!"

I didn't realize how chilly it was until I dropped Kathy off and headed home. Rounding the corner onto Wisconsin Avenue, I shuddered and my arms erupted in "goose bumps." My short-sleeved shirt was not enough to shield me from the cool night air. I wished I had her sweater. It was gonna be a long ride home! Then something brushed my knee.

Looking down, draped over the bar, was pink, shaggy warmth. I pulled over and unfolded the rug. It was just the right size to stretch over my shivering shoulders. It was wide enough so I could wad up a corner in each of my hands while I held the handlebars. The trembling stopped the moment I put it on. My teen ego was a little stressed, but I calmed it with the knowledge that it was two in the morning and everyone in Staples should be asleep.

Speeding down the street I could hear the two free corners of my rug flapping in the breeze. I watched the curious shadows that were cast on the road as I raced under the street lights. They were small when I was under the light, but grew large and long as I continued my trek.

The bizarre shapes played games with my imagination. They were strangely familiar, as if I had seen them before. The rug, whipped by the wind, resembled a cape. And did I see pointy ears on top of the head? The ears, head and muscular build could belong to only one man—could it be? Yes, it was the caped crusader. It was Batman on a bike!

Batman disappeared, along with the street lights, the moment I turned onto the shortcut through the railroad yards. The moon was gone, too. Crunching along the path, I reduced my speed and glared into the dark. When the crunching stopped, I turned my tire off the grass to get back on the path. It was hard to follow as it curved through the field. I didn't want to have an accident, nor did I want to encounter one of those things that goes bump in the night.

Pin holes of light in the dark ahead told of the distant depot. Soon the crunching sand gave way to a quiet ride on the board walk. Not wanting to tip my bike over again, I got off and pushed it to the depot parking lot before resuming my trip.

Passing the new water tower, I saw headlights coming my way. As the car grew closer, it slowed to a crawl, as if checking me out, and then kept going. Out of the corner of my eye I could see that it was black and white. "They're probably on their evening rounds," I thought.

The car turned at the intersection I had just crossed. I listened to see which way it turned. It was going around the block. I was going to see it again. I continued my pedaling and sure enough, there it was, waiting for me at the next intersection.

"Howdy," said a friendly voice from the car.

"Howdy." I answered, as I squeezed the hand brakes. Slowing to a stop, I stood beside my bike. Fumbling with the corners of the pink rug in my hands, I wondered why they had stopped me.

"It's pretty late to be out riding around. Where have you been?"

"I've been to a drive-in movie." Thinking that my answer needed further clarification, I added, "It was a Beatle's double feature."

Crickets chirped during the long pause.

"Where are you going now?"

My heart was pounding in my ears. Having never been stopped by the police, this was a whole new experience. Under the pink rug, my short sleeved shirt stuck to me like a second skin.

"I'm going home."

Another long pause. In a flash, those chirping crickets in the ditch became a stampede of buffalo in my head.

56

"Are you Pat Miller's son?"

"Yes, I am."

After a moment of silence, the car door closed and the car drove away.

Not knowing what to do, I adjusted my cape, got on my bike and raced home. Snuggling under the covers, happy I wasn't in jail, I drifted off to sleep. Truly, it had been a hard day's night for this Batman on a bike.

Cool mud oozed between my toes as we guided our canoe down the steep bank into the shallow water. The warm morning sun filtered through the maple trees promising it would be a good day.

Kathy had invited me to go with the youth group from her church on a one-day canoe trip down the Crow Wing River. Beginning at her folks' property, just upstream from Wah-hoo Valley, we'd enjoy five or six hours of paddling, drifting and soaking up the sun until we arrived at our destination: McGivern Park. That stretch of river winds lazily in and out of pasture lands and forest. In midsummer its average depth, not counting fishing holes, is a fun-loving two feet.

Ours was the third of six canoes to slide down the slippery bank onto the quiet water. The first was already gone, carried away by the strong current in the middle. The second was hung up in the bushes on the other side of the river. Amid loud cheers and applause from those waiting their turn behind us, the novice canoeists, in ankle deep water, pulled their craft from the bushes, pointed it down stream and resumed their journey.

Kathy's dad, Joe, held the canoe steady as we got in. Sitting in the rear, she'd rudder and up front, I'd provide power by paddling on the left. Our towels, cooler and munchies were on the canoe bottom between us.

Joe had hunted, fished and trapped along that river since he was a boy and since this was my first time on that particular stretch of river, I listened in as he gave Kathy some last minute tips:

"Hey, Kath, watch for rocks under the surface and stay away from overhanging trees. If you go under 'em they'll drag you out of the canoe into the water.

Be real careful when you get near Bullard's Bluff. You'll see an island in the middle of the river. When you see it, keep to the right. That side is shallow, slow and sandy. The left is narrow, fast and deep. The banks along that side are weak and some of the trees may have fallen into the water. The farmer who owns that land usually drags the trees out of the river when they fall, but you never know. The river changes every day. Have fun, see ya later."

Once on the river our paddles were silent as we dipped them into the silky water. Crickets chirped along the banks and the wind whispered in the pines. A buzzing horse fly circled my ear and then was gone. The bottom of the canoe was cool on my bare feet; the sun on my arms was warm. We had entered another world with the push of a paddle.

Coming from behind us, two canoes engaged in a race. Soon vigorous paddling turned into an explosive water fight that included everyone! The serenity of the river was blown away by the laughter and uncontrollable joy that only a mischievous youth group can generate. Within moments we were all soaked and smiling.

Racing and splashing continued as we made our way downstream until somebody yelled, "I'm hungry!" Rounding the next bend, we found the perfect dining room— a sunny sandbar. We pulled the canoes onto the sand and laid our soaked jeans and sweatshirts on them to dry.

Despite our plastic coolers and plastic bags, our sandwiches were drenched. But we were on the river and no one really cared. Rolling up our bologna and cheese like cigars, we munched and tossed soggy chunks of bread to the birds.

After lunch we got back into our canoes and let the river give us a free ride. An occasional nudge from a paddle was all that was required to keep the canoe on course. Dangling hands and feet in the water, everyone was quiet, soaking up the sunshine. Even the cloudless sky seemed to kick back and relax.

The canoes grew further apart and soon we were barely in shouting distance of each other. No one seemed to mind. Paddles were quiet. It was a sleepy afternoon and we savored every moment.

Pulling a couple cans of pop and a bag of red licorice from our cooler, I made my way to the back of the canoe to talk to Kathy. I folded up one of our towels and a partly-dry sweatshirt to sit on.

The river was wide, the current was slow and the pop was cold. Fumbling to open the bag of licorice, I thought I heard something. It sounded like wind in the trees—or was it rushing water? The sound seemed to be off in the distance.

"Are we near Bullard's Bluff?"

"I don't know. We're heading toward a bend in the river. It could be a piece of land or it could be an island. The water on the right side looks too shallow for a canoe to pass without getting stuck. I can't tell if it's the river going around an island, or just a bayou."

"It's probably just a bayou. Let's see what's around the bend." I opened the licorice and offered the bag to Kathy.

As we rounded the bend in the river, Kathy's' gasp and the sound of rushing water told me that we were in trouble. We were at the island, on the left side, heading to the place that Joe had warned us about.

I scrambled to get to my seat in the front and to find my paddle. The friendly, slow moving river that had been one hundred feet across only moments ago, was now hostile, swift and getting dangerously narrow. Soon we would find ourselves in a tight passageway of violent, white water and mangled trees.

"Is the river completely blocked?" I called to Kathy. "Maybe we could slip through an opening or under one of the trees."

"It's completely blocked. There is no way to get through. It's only twenty feet across and full of fallen trees. We've got to turn around."

The powerful current continued to drag us toward the noisy, hopeless tangle. I couldn't see the toppled trees, but their roar was close enough. Paddling furiously, we attempted to turn around in the narrow passage. Scraping its way through overhanging tree branches and long grass, the white water shoved our canoe into a tall, muddy bank.

Knowing better than to reach out and grab a handful of grass and dead branches on the bank, I reached out and grabbed a handful of grass and dead branches on the bank. The front of the canoe was now motionless, held in place by my adrenalin-charged death grip. That heroic move, of course, left Kathy's end of the canoe in the middle of the oncoming flood. In a flash the raging water capsized our canoe plunging us into the churning foam.

Snatching a quick breath of air, I was sucked under the water only to be thrown back, as if by unseen hands, and hung on a toppled tree. It was about a foot in diameter with half of it above the water and half beneath. With my arms on top, my chest forced against its side and the rest of me being pulled by the relentless current, I was a wet rag on a clothes line in a windstorm.

Fighting against the current, I wriggled my way to the mossy top side of the tree trunk.

"Kathy!" I shouted.

"I'm over here!"

"Are you okay?"

"I'm hanging onto some branches, but they keep breaking off in my hands!"

Helpful as a toad on the tree trunk, I glared into the mist and wished we'd stayed to the right.

The guys in the canoe behind us had seen us get dumped and were running along the bank to where we were.

"Kathy, Ken where are you?"

"I'm in the water!"

"I'm on a tree!"

They located Kathy and fished her out of the churning river. Next, they talked me off my slippery perch onto dry land.

Kathy and I hitched rides with our rescuers and started to look for our canoe. The search was a short one. The canoe and paddles had been found by some campers at Bullard's Bluff. Our cooler, towels, sweat shirts and jeans were gone.

I knew I was going to miss my favorite pair of worn-out blue jeans. But even more, I was going to miss my wallet. No, it held no money— it contained a souvenir—the first communication that I had received from my local draft board. I had been classified 1A!

Chapter 7

Crisis to Quest

We said our good-byes and the door to my dorm room closed. Listening to Mom's and Dad's footsteps going down the hall, I took a deep breath, plopped onto my bed and thought about the fact that I was now a college student and I was on my own. The realization was both exciting and frightening.

Earlier that summer, I had taken my list of textbooks to Lowell Lysaker, my counselor from Services for the Blind, to see which ones were available on tape through the SSB Communications Center. English and Mass Communications were, but Physics and Speech were not.

"In cases like this," he explained, "funding is available to hire another student in your class to read your text book to you."

As freshman, Kathy and I had registered for the same general studies classes; she was looking for a part time job; I needed a reader and Duane's House of Pizza delivered!

On two previous trips that summer, I had walked the campus, studying its terrain. With no depth perception, it was important to know where every curb, step and staircase was located. Tripping on curbs that weren't there and stubbing my toes on stairs that were, embarrassed me. But more then that, I liked the feeling of being independent and being able to get around campus without Kathy. There was no need for her to feel like my "Seeing Eye girlfriend."

Traveling from building to building was easy. Finding classrooms within those buildings was another story. The tops of the door frames were out of sight, so reading the little room numbers was impossible. Larger landmarks needed to be found.

Counting the number of doorways or water fountains down halls or past stairways seemed to work the best. Those objects didn't move and were easy to find. My English classroom was the second door on the right, after turning left at the bottom of the stairs. My physics class was on the third floor, second door on the left, after taking a right at the top of the stairs. I marked my psychology and computer science lecture halls the same way.

Once classes began, I found myself falling asleep listening to my English assignments. The books were long and there was no way to turn the speed up on my reel-to-reel recorder. That technology was a few years away. My algebra class drove me crazy and history was a struggle. Out of all the classes I had taken by the end of my freshman year, I enjoyed those that were in the mass communications department the most. They seemed to include all the things I enjoyed: radio, TV, electronic equipment and people. So I declared mass communications as my major and began to take classes that were required for a four-year degree in that field.

Kathy's older brother Charlie was attending Moorhead State at the same time we were and had invited us to his apartment for supper. I had a late class and Kathy went to his place earlier in the afternoon. He said he'd pick me up around six by the door at the south side of Holmquist Hall. The driveway was only a few feet from the building so it would be easy for me to spot the big light-colored-car shape as he drove up.

Six o'clock came and I was standing in the hallway looking out the door when a light-colored-car shape drove up the driveway and stopped in front of the door. Swinging the hall door open, I took a couple eager steps, opened the car door and jumped in.

As I closed the car door, my nose told me something was wrong. Instead of being greeted by the aroma of a man's cologne, I was surrounded by the pleasant fragrance of a woman's perfume. In that single moment, I knew two things: one, I was in the wrong car and two, when I turned to face the driver, it wasn't going to be Charlie.

Sitting behind the wheel of this light-colored-car shape, at six o'clock, my pickup time was, I think, a young co-ed. She appeared to be short in stature and had very long, light-colored hair. I could not see an expression on her face, but the tension in the car told me she probably wasn't smiling.

Imagining she'd not find it complimentary if I told her I had mistaken her for my girlfriend's brother, I mumbled a quick, "Excuse me," and got out of the car.

Relieved that I didn't get Mace in my face, I resumed my position inside the hallway door and listened as the light-colored-car shape backed out of the driveway.

Moments later another light-colored-car shape drove up the drive way and stopped in front of the door. A couple sluggish footsteps brought me to the car and my tentative hand opened the door.

From the inside of the car, Charlie asked me a one word question, "Hungry?"

Getting in and closing the car door, I gave a one word answer, "Yup."

I received word that our department chairman wanted to see me. Assuming it had something to do with textbooks or class schedules, I stopped by his office after my nine o'clock class.

"Good morning, Ken. Please sit down."

His voice was friendly, but sober.

"Since you have declared mass communications as your major, I thought we should sit down and talk."

He cleared his throat. "We are very happy to have you here at Moorhead State. During your time here you will learn and experience much. It will be a positive time of growth and development for you as a person. You will never regret working for—and receiving your degree. But I must be very honest with you, Ken—no one is going to hire you after you graduate."

Like a recorder suddenly put on pause, the world stood still. My stomach formed a fist and tears gathered behind my eyes. What did he just say? Then the playback began: "No on will hire you. No one will hire you. No one will hire you." The rest of his message that morning was drowned out by the tape: "No one will hire you."

Up to that point I had successfully held the haunting specter of my future at arm's length, not even glancing in its direction. Pushing the peas to the side of my plate had been working just fine. Now, in one sentence, a man I didn't even know had knocked my arm to my side, setting me face to face with my own personal Goliath.

What if he was right? He's probably right. He's the department chairman; he should know. Why would anyone want to hire me, anyway?

On the way back to my dorm room, the taunting began: "He's right. No one will hire you after you graduate. Why should they? Who wants to hire a blind journalist? Who wants a blind technician stumbling around the station spilling coffee and knocking equipment on the floor? You're a lot more trouble than you're worth. What are you gonna do now? May as well quit. You've got no future. Why don't you just go home?"Arriving at my dorm room, squeezing the headphones real tight, I put a Janis Joplin record on the turntable and turned the volume up. No one could sing the blues like Janis and at that moment in time, she was singing my song.

It took me a moment to realize the banging was not on the record. It was coming from my dorm room door. Turning the volume down, I could hear my neighbors' voice, "C'mon, Miller! One of the frats is having a party, we've got a car and we're goin'! Open the door or you'll be left behind!"

"Alright, already. I'm comin'! Hold your horses!"

Five or six anxious guys waited in the hall. Closing my door, we were headed for the parking lot.

Walking in the door of the frat house, my senses were bombarded by cigarette smoke, loud music and loud voices.

"Hi, Ken. Welcome to the party." A student I didn't recognize was handing me a glass of something cold and dark.

"Thanks, what's this?"

"It's a rum-and-Coke. You'll like it."

After my first sip, I knew he was right. As I finished the second drink, the sweet chill washed my department chairman's words far, far away. Then someone brought in the keg and it was time for a couple beers. Tom Sawyer, alphabetical order, Batman on a bike! Life was good again.

Even though its effects were only temporary, I found in alcohol an escape from the whirlwind of decisions and responsibilities that plagued me. By the middle of my sophomore year, the thought of my future still brought the battle, but I could always find the bottle.

She stopped reading and put the book down.

"Why do you keep looking at your watch?"

"Some of the guys are getting together tonight and I don't want to be late."

"We have a test tomorrow. Don't you care about your grade?"

"Not really."

"It's a waste of time for me to sit here and read this to you if you are not going to take it seriously."

"I know."

"So what should we do?"

"Let's quit. This is boring anyway."

"Well, I need to study for this class, too."

"So go study by yourself. No one is stopping you!"

Tensions in our relationship increased. She didn't like the guys I was hanging around and I didn't want to study all the time. We decided that we should stop seeing each other for a month or so. Perhaps, we reasoned, a few weeks away from each other would do us some good. Maybe we were just going in two different directions in life. Couples call it quits all the time. Why should we be any different? She may need to go her way and I may need to go mine.

The break up was exciting and scary at the same time. We had been together for over two years. We were in love. We had something special. I felt secure in the relationship. Yet somehow that security had turned to bondage. My new friends let me be me. But I still thought about her.

Our break-up had lasted several weeks when my phone woke me up one Saturday afternoon in late February. It was Kathy.

"Did I wake you up?"

"No," I lied, "what's up?"

"I wondered if you wanted to go to church with me."

Church, I thought, why would I want to do that? "I like to sleep in on Sunday morning."

"How about if we go to the Newman Center? They have mass at five on Sundays."

That sounded like a good compromise. I didn't have to give up my night out, and I could still be with Kathy.

We were not sure what to do at mass. It was not like any of the Lutheran or Methodist services we had ever been at. So we just observed what everyone else did and followed their example. When they stood up, we stood up. When they knelt, we knelt.

I wasn't getting anything out of the service until the priest read the gospel lesson for that day. It was one of the scripture passages where Jesus heals a blind man. Remembering those stories from Sunday school, I let my mind run with the idea of being sighted, but then snapped it back to reality.

We visited the Newman Center again the next week. Most of the service was identical to the week before, including a story about Jesus healing a blind man. This time, however, it was from a different gospel. The story was about a different blind man, but the result was the same. The man was healed.

This time, I gave my mind a bit more time to consider what it would be like to see. "If I could see-someone would hire…." But then I quickly "reeled in" my curiosity like a fisherman afraid his hook would get hung in the weeds.

During the weeks that followed, we visited several other churches. Each one represented a different denomination; each service was unique in its tradition and each pastor had his own style of preaching. But each Sunday the gospel lessons had one thing in common. Each one told of how Jesus related to the blind men with which he came into contact. He healed them all.

This was too weird. Different churches, different pastors, but the same message. Jesus opened blind eyes. We heard that message too many times to be dismissed as coincidence.

Was God trying to say something to me? Could God heal me? Would God heal me? I believed that Jesus performed miracles when He was here. Could he do it today—would he do it today, in 1972? Would He do it for me?

If He healed me, if I could see, everything would be different. Getting a job would not be a problem. The American dream would be easy to grab. I'd be able to drive my big fancy car to work. I'd be just like everyone else.

What if God was trying to get a message to me? What if He did want to heal me? He sure wasn't going to heal a party guy, so I set out to clean up my act.

Drinking and partying were first to go. Faithful attendance at church was now a priority. I wanted to show God that I was serious about getting healed. I told Him if He healed me, I'd serve Him the rest of my life!

Getting the phone on the third ring, I heard Mom's voice.

"Hi, Ken."

"Hi, Mom, what's up?"

"Do you remember Howard Olsen? I think he graduated from high school a couple years ahead of you."

"Vaguely."

"He was one of those students who spent a lot of time in the principal's office and at the police station. He helped introduce drugs into the high school.

Anyway, he's back in Staples to try and to make things right with the people that he wronged. When he came back from Vietnam he was really messed up from the drugs he used while he was there. He spent some time with some Jesus People in California and now he is having Bible studies in his house here in Staples. Maybe you would like to visit with him the next time you are home."

I had heard about these Jesus People on the news. Many were drug addicts, criminals and prostitutes that had been converted to Christianity. They were creating quite an uproar in many denominational churches because they emphasized the reality of Jesus Christ and were not interested in liturgies and traditions. Because of that emphasis, these society dropouts were not always welcome in traditional churches.

They could be identified easily by their long hair, torn blue jeans, large tattered Bibles, huge crosses around their necks and their boundless, uncontrollable zeal. They told anyone who would listen—and even those who wouldn't, "Don't get high on drugs, sex or booze. Get high on Jesus." With an uplifted hand, index finger pointing to heaven, they boldly proclaimed: "Jesus is the answer!"

The raised hand and pointing finger meant that Jesus was the one, and only way to God. This gesture irritated people from other religions and members of many Christian churches. The Jesus People, or Jesus freaks, as some folks called them, were thought to be narrow-minded and intolerant because of their fierce adherence to the one-way doctrine that they considered fundamental to their faith.

I knew I had to talk to Howard. Certainly the only one who could bring sight to my eyes was a living Jesus, and that's whom these Jesus People seemed to know.

Over the next few weeks we had several contacts with Howard and his wife, Myrna. My number-one question for them was about healing. We looked into the scriptures and found only affirmative answers and encouragement. Listening to tapes by some well-known faith teachers further confirmed what we had found in the Bible. It was clear from the tapes and scriptures that God wanted to heal me. The unanswered question was, "When?"

Dad called to let me know that Howard and some of the men from his church were going to the upcoming Methodist Men's Conference in Minneapolis. He wanted to know if I would like to join them. The speaker on Saturday night was going to be Oral Roberts.

My heart leapt for joy! This is it! If there was ever a man whom God could use to bring healing to my eyes, it was Oral Roberts. I could already hear his voice challenging me to reach out for a miracle. At last, I was going to see.

Two days before the conference, I called my dad to let him know when to pick me up at the bus stop.

"I'll be arriving around two—and I only bought a one way bus ticket. I won't need one for the return trip. I will be able to see. Can I borrow the Mustang to get back to Moorhead?"

"Son, when we get back from Minneapolis, if you can drive it—it's yours."

Taking the bus from Moorhead to Staples, I met the guys and we drove to Minneapolis by car. During the drive, Howard told me about a Jesus Rally that he was putting together with the Jesus People Church in Minneapolis. It was scheduled for the next weekend in the Staples High School cafeteria. He was going to make final arrangements on Saturday afternoon and wondered if I wanted to go with him. Being curious about these Jesus People, I accepted his invitation.

Waiting in the living room on Saturday afternoon, while Howard took care of the final details, I joined a group of eight or ten young people listening to a tape. It was by an Episcopal priest, Father Dennis Bennett. He was talking about the importance of having a relationship with a living Jesus, not just having a religion about a Jesus who lived long ago. He spoke of Jesus as if he were a personal friend. Those who were listening to the tape seemed to know exactly what he was talking about. As for me, I knew about Jesus from the Bible, Sunday school and church, but that was about it.

After the tape was finished, their discussion revolved around that relationship. I didn't get it. To me, being a Christian meant going to church, obeying the Ten Commandments and doing good things. Were these people actually saying that a living Jesus wanted a personal relationship with me? Were they saying that He wanted to be my friend? Continuing to listen, I realized these young people were talking about a Jesus that I did not know. They had something real, something that could not be defined, or denied. Whatever they had was deserving of investigation, but right now I was on a quest. Tonight I was going to see.

Chapter 8

No Turning Back

The evening meeting began with the singing of hymns. Familiar from childhood, I knew every word by heart. But as we sang, I noticed something peculiar was happening to me and to the way I was responding to the music. Lyrics that had been meaningless words and empty phrases were suddenly taking on new meaning, new energy, and new life.

Great is Thy faithfulness, O God my Father.
There is no shadow of turning with Thee.
All I have needed, Thy hand hath provided.
Great is Thy faithfulness, Lord, unto me!

Like slowly waking from a nap, I was aware something was going on-but I didn't know what it was. My five senses raced to identify this strange new "awareness." They were unsuccessful.

I didn't get it. I was still the same Ken, sitting in the same church, in the same pew, with the same guys, and yet, something indefinable was happening to me. And because of that indefinable something, I knew my life could not go back to the way it had been. Without invitation, a smile crept across my face.

The thump, thump, thumping of my heart drowned out most of what Oral Roberts had to say. But that was okay. My smile remained. I knew what was coming.

When he finished, he told us that he was going to do things a little differently than he had in the past. Instead of a healing line, he was going to have us pray for each other.

"I'm reading from James chapter five, verse sixteen," he said. *"Therefore confess your sins to each other and pray for each other so that you may be healed. The prayer of a righteous man is powerful and effective."*

He told us to choose a partner. Howard was sitting next to me and already knew my request. Closing my eyes, we began to pray. With a heart full of faith and expectancy, I knew that when I opened my eyes, like wiping the fog from a bathroom mirror, my world would be a whole new place.

Unleashing my mind, I imagined what I was about to see. Everything would be in razor sharp focus and in blazing, radiant color. The brilliant hues in the stained-glass windows would burn my eyes. The ornate detail in the oak wood-work around the altar would take my breath away!

Then, the best part, I'd look down the row of men and see my father. Our eyes would meet and he'd know immediately what had happened. I'd watch with 20/20 vision as the etchings in his face from years of questions and worry would be washed away by the power of pure joy. Leaping to my feet I'd run to him, throw my arms around him and yell as loudly as I could, "Dad, I can see!" When our prayer was finished, I opened my eyes. The world was the same smeared, colorless blur my closed eyes had shut out only moments before. My vision had not changed, I didn't get my miracle.

Time stood still. Like hearing the voice on the phone say, "I've got some bad news for you," I waited for the disappointment. I braced myself against the reality—I had not been healed. I waited for the anger, the feeling of betrayal. God promised in the Bible and He let me down! I waited for the resentment and the bitterness to set in. But the "bad news" never came. Instead was a quiet reassurance in that newly awakened part of me. What mattered was the fact that He is God and was on my side. What mattered was the fact that He loved and cared about me. What mattered was that, even though I didn't understand it, He was faithful.

In those moments, my priorities had shifted. While the healing of my eyesight was still important, it was now in second place. First, and most important, was that Jesus was real. Not only was He real, He was alive!

On our trip back to Staples, we tuned to KTIS, a Christian radio station in the Twin Cities. Wayne Peterson was playing Christian records, reading Bible passages and talking about Jesus. Listening intently, I wondered if I should narrow my major to emphasize broadcasting rather than print media. Maybe, I thought, I should consider Christian broadcasting as a career.

Back in Staples, I called Kathy to let her know what time to meet me at the Moorhead bus depot. And as long as she was on the phone, I told her about the weekend, too. My excitement was obvious as I told her of my new found relationship with Jesus. My joyous monologue was followed by a long silence on the other end of the line, then, in a very tentative voice Kathy spoke. "Umm, okay. I'll see you at seven. Is your mother there?"

"Yeah, here she is." I handed the phone to Mom.

"Hi, Kathy, what's up?"

"What's the matter with Ken? Has he been drinking?"

"No, not at all. But you better prepare yourself for his arrival. He's not the same Ken who left on the bus last Friday."

When I stepped off the bus, one look at my face told Kathy something had changed. Instead of my usual gloomy grimace, she was met with a genuine smile. It was the kind that comes from the bottom of a joyful heart, not from the bottom of an empty bottle.

"Ken, what has happened to you?"

"Honey, Jesus is real—wait till this weekend. It's gonna happen to you!"

"What's gonna happen to me?"

"Howard has arranged for the Jesus People Church to put on a rally at the high school in Staples next Friday, we're gonna go and it's gonna happen to you!"

She never did get a straight answer to her question, but my behavior caused an immediate conflict within her. Not only was her boyfriend talking and acting a bit crazy, but he was talking about Jesus all the time! She was puzzled by the contrast: the living Jesus he was talking about and the religion about Jesus she practiced.

Early the next morning she picked up her phone to hear my voice.

"Have you got any gold thread?"

It was quiet at the other end of the phone before she answered my question.

"I think so..." Then her voice became suspicious. "What do you want gold thread for?"

"Have you seen those posters that have a hand with the index finger pointing toward heaven and the words 'Jesus—One Way' written below the hand?"

"Yes, I've seen them..."

"Would you sew one on the back of my jeans jacket?"

"Where?"

"On the back of my jean jacket."

"But everyone will see it there!" she protested.

"Bingo! What could be better? Gold thread on a blue billboard!"

Inter-Varsity Christian Fellowship was having a sort of "spiritual empha-sis" week on campus. It included Bible studies in the student union and Christian musicians in the coffee house. Armed with my newly embroidered "Jesus jacket" I dragged Kathy to every event that IVCF had lined up. From Larry Norman in the coffeehouse, to Bible studies on the second floor of the union—we were there! Each time Kathy protested I told her to be patient; *it* was gonna happen to her next weekend.

Sitting in the fifth row at the rally, my mind and heart were pulled in three directions at once: first, it was wonderful to be around people who knew Jesus was alive; second, I didn't know how it could be done, but I wanted Kathy to know Him as I did; third, I was going to ask Him to heal my optic nerves.

At the end of the meeting, when the invitation was given, Kathy was one of the first to respond. One moment she was standing next to me, the next she had disappeared. Everyone had gone back stage and that's where I found her. She was sitting on the floor talking to one of the members of the singing group that had performed that night. Her name was Lois.

Kneeling next to Kathy, I took her hand and gave it a squeeze. Joy of joys, *it* was gonna happen to her!

"What can we pray about?" she asked Kathy.

"I need to know Jesus is alive."

Her attention turned to me. "And what would you like prayer for?"

Through trembling lips, I told her I wanted to see.

She put a hand on each of our shoulders and started to pray.

Even though it was like trying to contain ten gallons of gladness in a five gallon bucket, I kept my cool. I prayed quietly because I wanted to hear Lois' prayer, but the words felt strange in my mouth. They were unfamiliar to me. Next to me I could hear Kathy praying also, and her words were weird as well. Lois stopped praying and we both looked at her, wondering what was wrong. She was smiling. "It's okay. Keep praying," was all she said.

The three of us sat on the floor and poured our hearts out to a God who was no longer far away, cold and distant. He was right there with us. He was alive!

Leaving my TV production class, I heard a bright and cheerful voice behind me.

"Excuse me, are you a Christian?"

"Yes, I am." My ego puffed up a bit. Had she picked up a Christian vibe or something? "How'd you know?"

"The embroidery on the back of your jacket." I think she stifled a snicker. "My name is Patti. My husband, Todd, and I are having a Bible study at our place tonight; you're welcome to join us."

She gave me their address and we continued out of the building.

"What's your major?" I asked.

"Mass Communications."

"Me, too. You were in the front row, sort of hunched over. I was sitting a few rows behind you." Again, her voice smiled. "Were you catching a quick nap?"

"No." Now it was my turn to smile, "I have really poor eyesight. I was taking notes."

That evening at the study Todd gave me a GIANT PRINT New Testament. It came in three large volumes. The print was still too small to read without my magnifying glasses, but I thanked him for the Bible and appreciated his thoughtfulness.

Kathy and I felt very much at home with Todd and Patti and the group of eight to ten students at their study. Everyone was new to the faith and eager to discover what the Christian life was all about. Jim Sherry was the oldest Christian in the group. He had known Jesus for two years and we held his opinions in high esteem. It was difficult to imagine what it would be like to have been a Christian for two years!

Hungry to learn all we could, we devoured the Scriptures and passed around books and cassette tapes as fast as we got our hands on them. The series that caught my attention was a series on divine healing. They provided a logical, step-by-step method for me to follow to receive my healing. After hearing those tapes I knew it was all up to me. All I had to do was "claim" what was legally mine, spend more time in the Scriptures and watch my mustard seed faith grow until I could say to my blindness, "Be thou cast into the sea!"

As time went on, our small Bible study began to grow in numbers. The living room couch and chairs filled first. Next, students sat cross legged on the floor. Soon the kitchen and hallway were jammed, too. Nobody seemed to mind until we couldn't stuff one more person into Todd and Patti's apartment.

John Houglum, one of the guys in the study, lived in a nearby trailer court and offered to reserve the court's community room every Thursday night for our meetings. By this time, our attendance was near fifty and we accepted his offer gladly.

Comprised mostly of college students, we were a sincere, tireless group of young believers who loved to sing, worship God and study the Bible. Our meetings could run from seven to way past ten or eleven and still no one wanted to go home. Being together was way too much fun!

We were like a herd of happy sheep playing in a lush green meadow. Yet, there was one thing missing. We needed someone who could make sense out of the many things we didn't understand. We needed someone who could help answer our countless questions. We were looking for someone who could relate to us as young people, someone with whom we felt comfortable, someone who knew Jesus the way we knew Jesus. This little herd of happy college-age sheep needed a shepherd!

We decided to make appointments with some local pastors and see if they could help us. During our visits, we explained our situation and asked a theological question or two that we could not resolve ourselves. These pastors were very willing to talk to us and answer our questions, but most of them were already very busy tending to matters in their own congregations and did not have time to take on another commitment.

After we had finished our last visit, a small group of us gathered to compare notes and figure out what to do next.

"I'm confused," I said. "Each guy had a different answer to our questions. One says that we'll be *raptured* before the *tribulation;* another says we're gonna be *raptured* in the middle and another says we're in the *tribulation'* right now. Some say you must *speak in tongues;* others say you definitely should *not speak in tongues.* Some say you must be baptized in a tank, another says it's okay to be sprinkled. One says that I have been healed, it just hasn't been manifested yet; another says I need more faith; and, still another says I need to keep asking and not give up. Whom do we believe? What do we believe? I'm not sure I am comfortable with any of the guys."

The others echoed the same concern.

After several moments of silence, Brian Thompson spoke, "I know of a man who meets with a group of Lutherans in Fargo. Maybe we should contact him."

"Why?" I asked. "What's so special about him?"

"He lives here in Moorhead, but is a part of Daystar Ministries."

"What's that?" I had never heard of Daystar Ministries.

"I'm not real sure; I think it's just a group of Christians that are committed to doing the Lord's work and, oh yeah--they live in *community*."

"Community?" I asked. "You mean like hippies?"

"No..." He chuckled.

"Like monks in a monastery?" I continued my jesting.

"No, they are people, like us, only they pool their resources and trust the Lord to meet their needs."

"Sounds pretty strange to me. What else do you know about him?"

"Not much, but I know some of the people in his Friday night group and they really like him."

"What's his name?"

"Dave Pett. Should I call him?"

"Yeah. See if he could speak at our meeting next Thursday."

By the time the next Thursday night rolled around, we were all looking forward to meeting this man named Dave from Daystar.

After we finished singing and had heard a few testimonies, Brian introduced Dave. He had only spoken a few words and it was obvious that he was the right man for our little group. The room was silent; every ear was tuned to his voice, every heart open to hear the voice behind the voice.

His message was simple. He began by reading from 1 Peter 2:9-10 (NIV). "But you are a chosen people, a royal priesthood, a holy nation, a people be-longing to God, that you may declare the praises of him who called you out of darkness into his wonderful light. Once you were not a people, but now you are the people of God; once you had not received mercy, but now you have received mercy." He told us how Jesus wanted to come right into the middle of our messes, darkness and confusion and be our friend.

God's spirit breathed life into those words and there were few dry eyes in the place. Everyone could relate to what Dave had read. All of us there knew of the disorder and chaos in our souls. What we heard was a message of hope and God's unconditional love. That evening we caught a brief glimpse of His grace and mercy. It was incredible, almost impossible to believe that He would reach out to a "people in darkness," and make them "a people belonging to God".

We asked Dave if he would consider taking our rag-tag fellowship under his wing and meet with us every Thursday night. "Yes," he said with a twinkle in his voice, "I believe I'd like that."

The phone started ringing the moment I entered my dorm room.

"Ken, it's Brian. Do you remember the other day in the student union, when we were talking about Christian radio?" He sounded excited.

"Yeah, I remember."

"I just got off the phone with Betty Matthews from the Encounter House...."

"What's that?" I interrupted.

"It's like a Christian half-way house. Anyway," he continued, "they have been asked by KQWB-AM if they could produce a one half-hour taped radio program with music and testimonies about how Jesus has helped set them free from drugs and alcohol. It would be aired on Sunday mornings at eight and simulcast on their sister station, KWIM-FM. The show would help fill their FCC requirement for public service time."

"Where do I fit in?"

"They've got the music, people to give their testimonies and even some equipment. But they don't have anyone to put it all together on tape. *That's* where you fit in! I told her you would give her a call this afternoon. What do you think?"

"This is good," I said. "This is very good!"

When I called Betty and explained who I was, her glad response almost blew the phone right out of my hand. I could hear the wild cheers from others in the background. My call had made their day, and Brian's call had certainly made mine.

Twenty minutes later Brian and I arrived at the Encounter House, an old church building in south Moorhead. The Sunday school unit had been converted to sleeping rooms for the residents and an apartment for Betty.

Once inside, Betty introduced me to Cary Gwynn, a scruffy, long-haired Harley rider with a beard and a heart of gold. He was the ringleader and director of this crew of eager new radio personalities. Everyone involved was excited about the show and had already been brainstorming some great script ideas.

The equipment they had to use was a miscellaneous collection of microphones, tape recorders and a turntable. When we added a couple pieces from my collection, we had enough to do the show. We set everything up in the living room of my apartment the next day. That evening we started taping the first of fifty shows and "Truth of Truths" was born!

The sweet fragrance of the lilacs by the front steps drifted through the open window. I had just finished editing the latest installment of "Truth of Truths" and I was ready for a walk.

Outside the apartment, soft sunshine fell from a cloudless sky warming everything it touched. Walking around the block, I started thinking about Kathy. I thought about the gladness in her laughter, the music in her voice and the tenderness in her touch. I thought about the way I missed her when we couldn't be together. I thought about our future and I knew what I had to do. Turning around, I went back to my apartment and picked up the phone.

"Kathy, it's a great day outside. Do you have time for a walk?"

"Sure, but just a short one. I need to get back to the theatre. Rehearsal begins at two."

"I'm on my way."

Walking near the campus, we were shaded from the sun by the enormous elm and maple trees that lined the street. All around us the air was rich from the blooming vegetation in the neighborhood yards and gardens. I took her hand.

"I've been thinking about us," I began. "I've been thinking that we belong together." We stopped walking and I turned to face her. I paused a moment to see if I could sense whether she knew what I was going to say next. (I had been accused of being "infatuated" once before and I didn't want to repeat that little episode!) No "vibes" either way, so I took her other hand. Then my mind went blank.

Finally, after a couple moments of silence, she guessed I needed some prompting. "And..." Was she smiling?

"And...um," I took a deep breath. "Will you marry me?"

Without hesitation she answered, "Yes. Ken Miller. Yes, I will marry you!"

Thrilled beyond belief, we set the date for August 26, less than ten weeks away.

Chapter 9

Tugs of Wars

One of the books passed around our Bible study was <u>I Believe in Miracles</u> by Kathryn Kuhlman. In it she told of the many miracles that she had seen in her own life and in the lives of others. It was followed by her second, <u>God Can Do It Again</u>.

In addition to her writing, she was also known for her weekly radio and TV shows. Her ministry was all about miracles, faith and believing in the supernatural power of God. When I read her books, I thought, "Yes, I believe in miracles, too!"

At Bible study one night someone made the unbelievable announcement that Kathryn Kuhlman was going to be in the Twin Cities for one Sunday afternoon meeting. Once again, like wind on campfire coals, my desire to see was ignited and burst into flame.

My fingers spun the rotary dial as I called my folks to see if we could stop there on our way.

"Sounds great," Mom said. "You could stay here Saturday night and leave in the morning. How many will be coming?"

"I dunno, eight or ten."

"We have plenty of room downstairs."

Getting out of the car Saturday afternoon we were greeted by happy voices and smoke from the burgers on the grill.

After we finished supper we gathered in the living room and tuned up our guitars for a prayer and praise meeting. Everyone was full of faith as we sang, "God can do anything, but fail!"

Then someone said, "I think we should pray for Ken and thank the Lord for what He is going to do tomorrow." Everyone agreed and I pulled my chair into the center of the living room. I could feel hands on my shoulders as my friends gathered around me and began to pray. "Lord, we thank you for our brother Ken. We thank you for what he means to us. We thank and praise you in advance for what you are going to do in his life." Another continued, "Lord we know you are a God of miracles and know you came to give sight to the blind. We claim Ken's healing, right now, in Jesus' name!" And another, "Lord, it was because of your sacrifice on the cross, your 'stripes' that Ken is healed, and we thank you!"

The prayers continued for several minutes. I sat with my hands uplifted to the One I knew as my Lord and Savior, the One, who tomorrow, would open my eyes. "Lord, I thank you," I prayed, "that in Matthew 21:22, you said that if I believe, I will receive whatever I ask for in prayer. And Lord, I'm asking you, I'm asking you right now, to heal me, and I believe you will! Amen!"

As hands were lifted from my shoulders and everyone returned to their seats, I was overwhelmed by the love that these dear friends had for me.

The next morning I flew up the stairs to breakfast on angels' wings. Today was the day I was to receive my sight! I had found a pocket-sized Bible that I was going to bring along. It contained both the Old and New Testaments. The print was absolutely microscopic!

The moment I was healed I was going to run to the front of the auditorium. Holding that tiny Bible at arm's length, I'd read the story from John, chapter nine, about the blind man Jesus healed. Then I was going to shout at the top of my lungs, "Once I was blind, but now I can see! Praise the Lord God Almighty! I have been healed! I can see!"

We were an hour and a half early that Sunday afternoon so we could get a good parking spot and a seat close to the front. When we drove up to the entrance, the parking lot was already jammed with buses and cars. A multitude of people was standing in line outside the building waiting for the doors to open. The air was filled with the thick smell of diesel exhaust and the sound of expectant voices could be heard over the rumble of the bus engines. By the time we found a place to park, the doors had been opened and the people were pouring into the auditorium.

Inside the building the atmosphere was so saturated with hope and antici-pation that I could almost reach out and grab a handful! Everyone there was hoping to see miracles. They were looking to see supernatural wonders. Some, like me, were there seeking their own miracle; others brought friends who were in need.

The only people allowed on the main floor were those in wheel chairs or in hospital beds. Some were still hooked up to their IV's. Most of the seats upstairs were already taken. The only seats available to us were those in the far end of the building. Sitting in my seat, I could almost feel the breath of God blow across my face. This must be what it was like in Bible times, I thought, when people knew that Jesus was coming to town. A chill ran down my spine. There was no doubt in my mind that today was going to be the day I would see.

The music started and a song leader from the stage asked us all to join him in singing.

Shackled by a heavy burden

'Neath a load of guilt and shame
Then the hand of Jesus touched me
And now I am no longer the same

He touched me, oh, He touched me
And oh, the joy that floods my soul
Something happened and now I know
He touched me and made me whole.

Then a spotlight pierced through the dim auditorium and directed every-one's attention to the stage and Kathryn Kuhlman was introduced. I pulled the tiny Bible from my pocket and opened it on my lap.

"She's dressed in white," Kathy whispered in my ear. "The sleeves of her dress are full length, and they're cut wide at the wrist. She looks like an an-gel."

The air was charged with electric expectation as Kathryn spoke to the crowd. As if directed by God Himself, she began to call out various diseases that were plaguing people in the audience. She'd name the disease and then name the particular section of the auditorium where the healing was taking place. People on the floor were getting up from their wheel chairs. Others claiming healing from cancer and other diseases were making their way to the stage to tell of their miracle.

I knew it wouldn't be long before she would be calling out our section. I tightened my grip on the Bible in my lap. Then I heard her say it, "You people in the back...." Through anxious tears I stared at the little Bible. With each blink of my eye I looked foreword to viewing a whole new world.

"You people way in the back, way in the back of this huge building...." At last, it was my turn! I waited for the words, "God is healing someone who has been blind from birth." But instead, she said, "God is healing someone with arthritis." She had barely finished her sentence when a very elderly woman in the row in front of me struggled to her feet and shouted, "I'm healed!" Then Miss Kuhlman went on to call out healings in other areas of the auditorium.

I was crushed; I didn't understand. I didn't want to seem disrespectful to God or anything, but to me, it didn't make sense. Here I sat, a young man with my whole life ahead of me. I had believed that I would be healed. All my friends believed, too. Why then did this older woman get healed, and not me? It didn't seem fair. I thought I had the faith that I needed. I wiped the tears from my eyes and put the little Bible back in my pocket.

After the service, the ushers had us wait for a few moments while some hospital beds and wheel chairs were moved past our exit. No one spoke as we filed out of the auditorium. No one knew what to say. By the time we got back to Staples, it was too late to return to Moorhead, so we spent the night.

The next morning, the wings of gladness that had carried me up the basement stairs were now feet of clay. The light dancing footsteps of the morning before were now heavy and dull. My emotions were frayed like an old tattered rug.

No words were spoken at the breakfast table, but hearts were noisy trying to understand the day before. The unspoken questions were, "Why? Why wasn't Ken healed? Why hadn't God answered our prayers? Didn't we have enough faith? What had we done wrong?"

The title of the course was Mass Communications Law. The text book, four inches thick and as heavy as a small truck, was full of large words and small print. It was not available on tape or in large print so a reader needed to be found.

Kathy was involved in her own studies toward her degree and did not have time to spare. I did have one other option –our friend, Patti.

We decided to study at her apartment in the afternoon while her son, Chad, was taking a nap. But just about the time we'd figure out how to pronounce one of those long Latin terms, Chad would wake up and our studying would end.

When given the choice between listening to a less-than-exciting law book and playing with Chad—there was no contest. In the twinkling of an eye, Chad became the world's greatest cowboy and I became the world's wildest buckin' bronco!

Usually, somewhere in the middle of the thumping and bumping of our rodeo, Todd would return from his accounting class. Then he and Patti would start the evening meal. Soon I was on the phone to Kathy conveying their invitation to join them for supper.

Two guys from our Bible study, David and Dean, lived in the same building and they'd get an invitation as well. Afterwards we'd go to the living room and philosophize about school and the Christian life.

Shared meals and evening discussions at Todd and Patti's became a tradition! And, to reciprocate, Kathy and I would invite everyone over to our apartment for the same.

One evening we found ourselves talking about the amount of money we were paying for rent and utilities on our three apartments. Todd's calculator was close by, so just for fun, we added up those figures. The grand total started the brainstorming session.

"Hey, I've got an idea." I said. "If Daystar can live in community, why can't we? We're together all the time anyway, and it sure would be economical."

Everyone saw the financial advantages of such a venture, so we started to look for a place where we could all live together.

We heard a rumor that Daystar was going to buy the building that formerly housed the Encounter House. That meant that the house that Dave was now living in would be available for rent. This could be our opportunity to try out community living, and save some money in the process!

The two-story structure was in an older neighborhood in south Moorhead, near the river. It had a huge pine tree in its small front yard. Kathy told me the house was painted green. Inside, the beautiful hard wood floors and oak woodwork made it a very attractive place to hold small Bible studies and get-togethers.

Dave confirmed the rumor. He said he didn't think our renting it would be a problem. After a few phone calls, the arrangements were made and our little community was given the okay to move into what we called the Green House.

Todd, Patti and Chad had the two rooms on the second floor for bedrooms. Kathy and I took one of the bedrooms on the ground floor and David and Dean shared the other.

To be certain there was no confusion for the neighbors about the nature of this little community, we posted a three-by-four foot metal sign in the front yard between the sidewalk and a huge pine tree. It said, "JESUS CHRIST, AMERICA'S ONLY HOPE."

We divided up some of the household responsibilities. Kathy and Patti bought the groceries, Todd took care of the finances and I appointed myself as spiritual leader.

Needless to say we had our share of conflicts. We could never see eye to eye on such matters as which type of milk should we use--skim or whole; which should go on our bread, margarine or butter; how can we divide food costs fairly when we all have such different schedules?

We didn't always agree on my spiritual authority either. I did manage to *inspire* those in our house to accompany me to the West Acres Shopping Mall to hand out tracts, but generally my great ideas were met with a less than enthusiastic response.

Listening to a tape one afternoon from one of the Jesus people groups in California, I stumbled across what seemed to me, to be a unique way of spreading the good news. With gospel tracts jammed in pockets, one of these young evangelists would go into a public rest room; enter a stall and unroll ten or twelve feet of toilet paper. Then, while rolling it back up, they'd place individual tracts on the paper about three feet apart, so the next occupant would have something to read. Other ideas from the tape sent my mind spinning so I told everyone we'd have a short meeting that evening to discuss our next trip to the mall.

David and Dean had school and work responsibilities so they couldn't come. Meeting time came and went and Todd and Patti didn't show up. When I went to investigate, I found them in the back yard giving Chad a hair cut! When I reminded them about the meeting, they told me they didn't want to come. Unaware of the existence of that option, I moped my way back to the house and picked up the phone.

It seemed that we were always having little issues popping up that would require a visit from Dave; he was the only one we'd all trust when it came to making decisions.

The meetings made me crazy because Dave never saw things my way. I'd have a perfectly good agenda set up, but instead of going over *my* list and validating *my* authority, he'd talk to us about loving one another and getting along, even though we may be different from one another. Now, love is fine and all, but that's not what I wanted him to say.

While I was learning about love and leadership in my own little corner of the world, the Jesus Movement was sweeping through mainline denominational churches. Doctrinal walls that had separated Christians from one another for years were being breached on a regular basis. People were spending time having fellowship based on their relationship with Jesus, rather than spending time arguing about doctrine.

One summer weekend, my parents asked Kathy and me if we wanted to go with them and some others from their Methodist church to a meeting in St. Cloud at a Presbyterian church. We eagerly accepted their invitation. Being with other people who loved the Lord as we did was always on the top of our Things We Love to Do list.

The guest speaker's message could have been titled, "Faith, and How to Believe God." His presentation was methodical, logical and based in scripture. He said that if we followed this "road map," it would lead us to our miracle. I listened intently as he moved through his message one step at a time. He paid particular attention to faith's number one enemy: doubt.

When he was almost finished, to help illustrate his point, he told us about some of the miraculous things happening in his home congregation and challenged us to believe God for miracles in our own lives.

His words stirred my heart's desire to see God heal me. Here was a man of faith who had seen God actively involved in the lives of his friends. They had believed God for miracles and God had caused those miracles to happen and those prayers to be answered.

After the meeting was over, I asked him if I could have a moment of his time.

"Sure," his voice was kind and sincere. "How can I help you?"

"Would you pray for me?" I asked. "Specifically, for my eyesight."

"I'd be happy to." He bowed his head and placed his hand on my shoulder. "Lord Jesus," he began, "I'm asking you..." Then he stopped, lifted his head and spoke to me. "I don't know what this means. But, in my mind's eye, I see a picture of a car battery, wire and headlights. The battery is fine, the headlights are okay, but the wires that connect the two are broken. Does that have any significance to you?"

My heart jumped for joy. My mind filled with fireworks--like it was the Fourth of July! Yes, it most certainly does have significance! The fact that a total stranger sees a picture of broken wires is more than significant. It's a miracle!

I hadn't told him anything about my optic nerves, yet he had seen the precise source of my vision problem in picture form. The hair on the back of my neck stood straight up! How did he know? The only possible answer was that God must have told him.

I looked up and said, in a coarse whisper, "Those broken wires are my optic nerves."

Then, in a voice full of confidence he said, "And the Lord wants you to know that He is healing you right now."

Right now? My insides were flooded with expectation and gratitude towards God. Right now means right now! I was being healed "right now!" It didn't mean tomorrow or next week. It didn't mean yesterday. It meant right now! At last I was going to see, "right now!" But when I looked around the room, everything was the same. My eyesight had not changed.

My feelings of exhilaration were clouded by the reality of what I saw. My vision was the same as it had been before "right now" had begun! How could I bridge the gap between what he said, and what I saw?

The only way I could reconcile the conflict was to assume that this must be either a test, or one of those times we must "take it by faith". I didn't want to doubt, that would ruin everything! I had to believe I was healed, even though I saw no change. Yet this man, with supernatural insight, said the Lord was healing me "right now". So I started to watch and wait.

It was after dark when we left the church. We decided to go to Perkins and have a treat before driving back to Staples. From the back seat I eagerly watched the road ahead of us. I waited for the signs to suddenly snap into focus. I waited for the crystal clear spectacle of the bright colorful city lights as they blinked and flashed for miles ahead. I waited for the undefined shadows around me to become tangible substance.

I was still waiting when we drove into the Perkins parking lot.

Our waitress led us to our table on the other side of the restaurant. We passed tables on the right and booths to our left. On the other side of the booths were large windows that looked out into the night. I knew the shadowy movement I saw in their reflection was our hungry crew ready for some goodies.

As we sat in the restaurant, I kept eyeing the busy pattern in the carpet, waiting for it to burst into color.

Dad leaned over and asked, "Notice any change?"

"No, not yet," I didn't want to doubt! It was only a matter of time.

Our waitress brought our desserts. I could see no change in my eyesight, but the hot fudge sundae was yummy!

We all continued to laugh and talk and enjoy one another's company. I knew I was going to be healed. My faith was strong, but I still couldn't see any change in my sight.

Twenty minutes later our waitress came to pick up our dishes and there was still no change. But I held onto my faith. God said it, and I believed it! I had to believe. There were no other options.

I looked at the floor once again. I strained to detect the smallest improvement in my sight. There was none. Looking up, I longed to see my reflection in the windows I knew were across the restaurant. What a thrill that would be!

Back in the car on the return trip to Staples, I continued to look out the window, but I wasn't quite as enthusiastic about my healing as I had been before we stopped. What had happened? I always thought that "right now" meant "right now." But in this case, "right now" was becoming a very long time. Maybe, I reasoned, things will be better tomorrow.

When I awoke the next morning, my heart was filled with clouds. Why was this happening to me? I felt as if forces greater than I were having a tug-of-war, and I was the rope! On one arm I felt the pull of my own personal conviction that God was very much alive and that his love was unchangeable and aimed right at me. Unanswered questions were pulling the other arm. Why wasn't I healed? If

He really loves me, why tease me with empty promises? Why are some people's prayers answered immediately, and mine seem to be ignored?

Mom and I were the only ones in the kitchen. Sitting down at the table, I poured myself a glass of milk.

"Mom?"

"Yes, honey."

"Why wasn't I healed?"

"I don't know." She poured herself a cup of coffee and sat down across from me. "Sometimes God's ways are not our ways, and His thoughts are not like ours. He is God. We can't tell God what to do, or when to do it. Sometimes all we can do is trust that He knows what is best for us."

"But what about last night? That man saw a picture of..."

"I know," she interrupted. "I know what he saw and I know what he said. I don't know why you were not healed." She sipped her coffee before she spoke again. "Did you happen to see the Billy Graham crusade the evening that his guest was Joni Eareckson?"

"No, I missed it. Who is she?"

"She is a young woman who was paralyzed from the neck down in a diving accident at age seventeen. She talked about some of the things that she has learned about herself, God and suffering since her accident."

"Suffering?" I didn't understand. "Didn't Jesus come that we could have life, 'and life more abundantly?'"

"Yes, he did. But at the same time, things happen in our lives that we don't understand. Take Paul's 'thorn in the flesh', for example. Paul asked the Lord to take it away--three times. The Lord did not remove the "thorn". Instead He told Paul that His grace was sufficient. He said that His strength was made perfect in Paul's weakness. Despite the fact that God did not remove the "thorn", Paul's faith and devotion to his Lord remained as strong as ever."

I heard her words, but the tug-of-war in my heart continued.

Chapter 10

Destination Daystar

Nearly every weekend during the summer of 1973, Kathy and I packed our little purple Gremlin and drove to Zion Harbor, Daystar's family camp on Leech Lake. Almost all of the way there, we'd sing scripture songs and gospel choruses. Even though the trip took a bit over two hours, it seemed it only took a tune or two and we were on the bumpy corduroy road that floated on the swamp between Zion Harbor and Federal Dam.

It was always dark by the time we reached Zion, but we could hear joyous singing coming from the lodge building. The meeting was already in progress. Outside the frogs and crickets were raising their own song to heaven.

Despite the large crowd inside, there always seemed to be one parking spot left outside the front door. As our car pulled to a stop and the crunching of the rocks under our tires ceased, I could hear the words from inside, "I was glad when they said unto me, let us go into the house of the Lord." My heart soared like an eagle because I, too, was glad to go into His house.

After the meeting we'd stop at the registration desk. We didn't own a tent, but Gene Carlson always seemed to find a room for us for the weekend.

Lunch was over and we had gone outside to enjoy the sun. Waves rolled onto the beach, then hissed quietly as they retreated back into the lake. Sea gulls squawked as they fished when a man sat down next to us and introduced himself.

"Excuse me, are you Ken Miller?" he asked.

"Yes, I am."

"My name is Jon Lyle." A blur of movement between us told me that he had extended a friendly hand.

"Pleased to meet you, Jon." I shook his hand.

"I am in charge of the cassette tape ministry here at camp. I understand that you have an interest in electronics and, well...." His voice grinned, "I'd like to show you what we're doing here at Zion and see if you have any ideas or suggestions for us."

"Sounds good to me." I didn't want to sound too eager, but my insides were churning with excitement.

On the way to our first stop, the tape room, Jon said that each message given during the camp was recorded, duplicated and made available for sale in the camp bookstore or through a catalog that was being put together. The tape room was actually two rooms: the first and larger of the two was where the tapes were duplicated, labeled and boxed; the second room was where the reel-to-reel tapes were edited and put on cassette masters for duplication. Jon introduced me to Bernice who was busy getting ready to mail out the "Tape of the Month". Next, we went to the lodge to see the public address and recording system in use there. All of the equipment was concealed in a cabinet near the back of the meeting hall. It had been made from the same tongue-and-groove boards that covered the interior of the building.

I found myself drawn to the whole concept of working in a Christian tape ministry. I let my imagination go for a moment. Being surrounded by recording equipment and fellow Christians sounded like the next best thing to heaven! Everything I had learned on my own and in school seemed to apply here. Working in that kind of environment would be a perfect fit.

Intrigued by the tape ministry and the community lifestyle, I asked Jon about what it meant to be a staff member of Daystar Ministries. He gave us some history and told us of Daystar's emphasis on Christian growth. Then we moved on to the more practical aspects of the ministry. That's when the wind ceased blowing in my sails. He told me that being on staff was a big commitment: the staff was not paid, but room and board were provided.

Returning to Moorhead Sunday afternoon, I tried to put the matter out of my mind. To be on staff would be an awfully big commitment. (What do I do if I want a Snickers bar?) Still, I was deeply impressed by the maturity I saw in some of the staff members. I envied the relationship I saw that they had with Jesus. Finances would be a real struggle, but on the other hand, it would be such a joy to serve God in such a sold-out way.

90

The fall of 1973 was approaching. With the change of seasons, we were also experiencing change at the Green House. Almost everyone knew what they were going to do at the end of the summer. Dean was going to Vienna to continue his studies; David was going to help his father in their family business; Todd, Patti and Chad were returning to Hibbing. But, like leaves that would soon be tossed around yards and streets by the wind, Kathy and I weren't sure what was ahead.

I had seen the schedule for the fall classes that were being offered at MSC, but I was having a hard time getting excited about them. Kathy's level of enthusiasm for her fall classes was equally low. We found ourselves being drawn more and more to our new friends, and the sense of belonging that we found in Daystar. We began to seriously and prayerfully consider the possibility of being part of that ministry.

So I asked Dave how we could become members. He told us that all we had to do was write a letter to the ministry staff. The letter should contain information about us and why we wanted to become a part of Daystar. Our letter would be read and brought up for a vote at a staff meeting at Zion Harbor. If it seemed that we understood and agreed upon what Daystar was all about, we would be invited to become part of the ministry; the vote had to be unanimous.

"If you are received on staff," he said. "You will probably move to Zion Harbor. Jon could use some help in the tape room and Kathy, you could be a big help in the Christian school we are starting in Federal Dam."

Kathy and I spent many hours that summer walking the streets of Moorhead wrestling with our options. But, after much careful consideration, we wrote our letter and gave it to Dave. Then we started to wait for a response.

Goose bumps erupted on my arms as I pedaled across the bridge between Fargo and Moorhead. I had been in Fargo listening to a rock 'n' roll band. They had asked me to record their demo tape, but I wanted to hear them before making a commitment.

It was already after dark as I turned off Main and headed south on the one-way that ran along the Red River. Even though the route was unfamiliar, I felt confident that I could find my way home. All I had to do was count street corners. How hard could that be?

Turning onto the one-way, I noticed something immediately. The street was not very well lit. Maybe, I reasoned, there were fewer street lights than normal, or maybe my eyes had not yet adjusted from the bright bridge lights. But whatever the reason, the dark made the driving uncomfortable. I didn't want to hit a parked car, nor did I want to get hit by a moving one. At that point, my only option was to grit my teeth, glare at the black void in front of me and hope for the best.

Occasionally a car would race past making the shadows around me dance as if they were cast from some mysterious campfire. I counted the blocks at each intersection. "One, two, three...oops here comes a car, better pull over." Standing by the edge of the road, the heat from its engine warmed my hand. "Hey, driver," I thought. "You blind or what? You almost hit me!' Fussing about people who should not be driving at night, I got back on my bike and resumed my journey. "Four, or was this five? Rats, I don't remember!"

In the middle of the next intersection, I noticed something odd about the street. It was missing. Looming tall in the darkness ahead of me was a large building that, I assumed, belonged to the Concordia College campus. That meant I had gone several blocks past my turn. In fact, I must have made some real goofy turns because the campus was not even close to the road I thought I was on!

Turning my bike around, I headed back the way I had come. I could have stopped and asked someone for directions, but the hour was late and all the houses seemed dark on both sides of the street.

I rode a bit farther and a smirk twisted my lips as I mused over what I would say if I did stop. "Excuse me, I know it's late and I apologize for waking you, but I am in a predicament. You see, I was biking home and I got lost and I'm blind so I can't read the street signs to give me direction. Could you tell me where I am?" My face stretched into a full blown grin as I tried to imagine their response.

Be that as it may, there was no denying my present problem: I was lost. I knew that I could spend the whole night just riding up and down the street like a little lost puppy, but that wouldn't help me get home. I had to do something.

At the next corner, I stopped my bike and listened. The late night silence was broken only by the rustle of leaves in the trees and an occasional honk from the highway.

The next corner, on my backward trip, had a street light. Searching my surroundings for anything that might jog my memory and give me a clue as to my location, it caught my eye. Gleaming in the light of the streetlamp was something tall and narrow. Could it be a pole, a sign pole?

I reached out my hand to investigate. It was round, maybe four or five inches in diameter. It had to be a street-sign support. At the top of that pole was a sign with wonderfully written information that would tell me where I was! The only problem was that the wonderfully written information on that sign was not visible from where I stood.

Since I couldn't read it because it was mounted too high, there was only one option open to me. Grabbing the pole above my head with both hands, I pulled myself upwards. Then wrapping my legs around the pole to secure my position, I moved my hands farther up the pole and pulled again. After repeating this action three or four times, I found myself face to face with a wonderfully informative sign. In five inch letters the sign told me I was at the corner of Sixth Street and Eighth Avenue.

Before I began my descent back to earth, I heard a car door open just across the street. My stomach tightened. What would I say if that person were to cross the street and ask me what I was doing? What if the person in the car was a police officer? What if I was breaking a city ordinance that prohibits sign climbing? Would they believe me if I told them the truth? Or perhaps they wouldn't say anything, but wonder to themselves about which controlled substance I had ingested. My flushing face warmed my white knuckles.

The car door slammed and footsteps faded as the driver crossed a yard onto a porch. Moments later the jingle of keys and the closing of a door told me I was alone on the street again. Releasing the choke hold I had on the pole, I slid to the ground.

Now that I knew where I was, it was easy to find my way back to Seventh Avenue and home.

A month had passed and we were still waiting for a response to our letter. One Sunday morning after church, I asked Dave if he had heard anything.

"Oops," he chuckled. "Wait a minute."

He took a magazine from a nearby table and tore out one of those postage paid response cards. Then I heard his ball point pen click and he wrote something on the card and handed it to me.

"This should do for now," his voice was still smiling. "I need to get going; we'll talk more later."

With that, he was gone. Kathy looked at the card. In the corner he had written two words above his signature: "You're in!"

Chapter 11

A Perfect Fit

Leafless trees filtered the October sun casting long, late afternoon shadows across Zion's campground. Once again I heard the rocks crunch under our tires as our car drove up to the lodge. The air was crisp and clean and full of promise.

All of our earthly possessions were squeezed into our little purple car, including some new flannel shirts for me, a couple new outfits for Kathy, a very large tube of toothpaste and an enormous bottle of shampoo!

Inside the building I could smell supper cooking in the kitchen and caught an occasional whiff of smoke from the fire that crackled in the wood stove. Folks were already gathering around the buffet tables waiting to sing "Come and dine," the prelude to food! Outside, a ringing bell signaled supper for those who were in other buildings or working in the woods.

Jon Lyle and others we knew greeted us with warm, "welcome" hugs and happy voices. We joined the others in line and I squeezed Kathy's hand. I knew we had made the right decision to join Daystar. Like my best pair of faded blue jeans, it was a perfect fit! After supper, Oliver Carlson, the camp director, read devotions from Oswald Chamber's book, Streams in the Desert, and then we were dismissed.

"Hi, Ken and Kathy, welcome to Zion." It was Gene, Oliver's wife. "We have a room for you across the channel in the green house. It has a bed, dresser and desk. If you need anything else, please let me know." We thanked her and took our car on the dark dirt road that lead to the green house.

Doug McCoy greeted us and offered to help move our stuff into our room. He and his wife, Naomi, had a room down the hall from ours. We accepted his invitation, even though I knew it wouldn't take long to move us in. How much stuff can you pack into a Gremlin, anyway?

The next evening Kathy and I were browsing through the camp bookstore. As she read me some of the titles, I noticed that many related to faith and physical healing. These books had been authored by some of the big names in the "faith" movement. I bought several of the books with the intention of studying them closely in my spare time. Perhaps one of them held the key that would change my world.

Returning to the green house, we invited Doug and Naomi to our room for popcorn. Doug said he'd bring something special for us to drink. When they arrived he produced a one gallon jar filled with a dark liquid.

"What's in the jar?" I asked. I knew that the kitchen was out of Kool-Aid and pop didn't come in jars.

"It's sumac juice! You're gonna love it! I made it myself." His voice was full of pride and eagerness to share this Zion Harbor treat.

"S-sumac!" I stumbled over the word. "Won't that stuff make you sick?"

"No, no," he assured me, "this kind won't. It grows by the road just outside camp." I heard the "glug, glug" as he filled our glasses. "Here try it!"

I took the glass from him and raised it to my lips. I didn't want to seem suspicious in front of my enthusiastic friend, but I had never heard of sumac juice. On the other hand, I knew of his love for the outdoors and could certainly trust his judgment when it came to discerning the difference between good and bad sumac. So I gathered up all my courage, took a deep breath—and waited for Kathy to try hers!

"Mmm, this is good!" she said. "It's a little tart, but actually pretty good!"

With her endorsement I took a tentative slurp. Wonder of wonders, she was right; it was a bit snappy, but quite tasty!

When we finished our "taste tests" and had shared some laughs and popcorn, I asked Doug what he thought about physical healing.

"I don't really know what to tell you," his tone became serious. "Last summer we had a real powerful faith teacher here for camp. He got everyone real fired up to 'believe God to heal their eyes.' Everyone threw their glasses off the bridge into the channel as a 'step of faith.'"

"What happened then?"

"Well, the next week everyone crowded the bridge trying to fish their glasses from the channel. They couldn't see to do their work without them."

The next morning I attacked my responsibilities in the tape room like David running at Goliath-and this time, I was going to win!

My first Job was already waiting for me. I was to finish the master cassette for this month's "Tape of the Month." I closed the door to the small production studio behind me and sat down in the chair facing the equipment. I reached out to touch the cold metal front of the reel-to-reel tape deck and slowly manipulated the silky smooth volume control on the mike mixer. "This is it," I said to myself, "there is no place on earth I would rather be."

The squawking alarm from the clock radio on my nightstand made me jump. It was time to get cleaned up and go over to the lodge for breakfast. I pushed back the covers and sat up. Something was wrong. I felt awful.

That little cold I had been dodging had tackled me and was hosting a rock concert between my ears. The stomping stage was located right behind my eye balls and the drummer insisted on pounding out his throbbing rhythm on my sinuses until I thought they would explode! There was no doubt about it; I was caught in the merciless tentacles of a classic Minnesota winter cold! I pulled the covers over my head and went back to sleep.

Moments later I woke up when I heard our bedroom door close. Kathy had brought me some hot lemon tea and a piece of cinnamon toast. I sipped some of the hot tea, hoping that it would cut through the sludge in my throat.

"Jon says the 'tape room' will survive just fine without you and that they will pray for you at morning prayers." Her voice was cheerful. "Someone from the kitchen will bring you lunch. I have to go to school, see ya!" With that she gave me a kiss on the cheek and was gone.

I took another sip of tea and a couple bites of toast. The tea was warm and comforting on my throat. The toast took care of that empty feeling in my stomach.

I lay back in bed and thought about my situation. I had two options: I could roll over and go back to sleep, or I could use the time to check out the books and tapes we bought in the bookstore. Thus far, I had not been successful in my quest, but I knew it was only a matter of time before I found the missing piece to my puzzle. I was going to be persistent, like the widow in Luke 18:1-5, who kept after the judge until he gave her what she wanted.

I gathered all the tapes and books that we had collected on the subject and placed them on my bed, along with my magnifying glasses and tape player.

The early morning sun was pouring in the south and east windows giving the room a warm glow. Despite my cold, I felt that it was going to be a good morning. Snuggling under the warm blanket, I pushed the play button and began to listen. The speaker combined teaching from the Bible on healing with glowing testimonies of people who had experienced real miracles in their lives. His approach was similar to other messages I had heard about faith. Nevertheless, I was inspired by his stories of miracles and answered prayer.

The books were more difficult to deal with, since I could only read four to five letters at a time. But this was a topic that I was keenly interested in, so I pushed ahead anyway.

One book said that it was never God's will for us to be sick. We should always approach God with the confidence that He wants to heal us. It went on to say that I could "claim" my healing because of what Jesus had done on the cross. It quoted Isaiah 53:5: "But He was pierced for our transgressions, He was crushed for our iniquities; the punishment that brought us peace was upon Him, and by His wounds we are healed." I had heard another man say that it's like an inheritance check for a million dollars. It won't do you any good unless you take it to the bank, endorse it and "claim it".

When it came to faith, it suggested that I memorize scriptures relating to miracles and healing. It said that memorizing would help strengthen my faith. It quoted Romans 10:17: "And faith comes by hearing, and hearing by the word of God." To help my "faith" grow even faster, it provided a list of important scriptures for me to memorize.

Like David, who killed a lion and a bear before he went up against Goliath, I thought I should gain some "spiritual muscle" by defeating this cold rather than going after my eyesight. I started to memorize those scriptures that applied to my immediate situation to make them a part of me. I "claimed" my healing and lay my aching head on the pillow to rest and fell asleep.

I woke up when I heard the door to my room close. I didn't think I had slept long, but I could smell the chicken noodle soup someone had just brought me. They had set the tray on the stand next to my bed. I could hear their footsteps going back down the hall. As I raised myself on one elbow to see what else was on the tray, I noticed my throat was sore and dry, like I had swallowed some sand paper and a dozen dust balls.

I had expected to wake up feeling better. Then I recalled counsel from one of the books. "This is just a minor set back," I thought. "The devil doesn't want me to get better so he is trying to make me discouraged. These symptoms are just one of his lies!"

I finished my soup and lemon tea and then went back to the books and tapes. With the addition of this sore throat, I was more determined than ever to find my miracle. I found the list of scriptures and the list of steps, and began to study them all again. I was going to be victorious! The devil wasn't going to push me around!

A few minutes later, I felt my sinuses fill and begin to overflow! The cold was getting worse not better! The books told me that when that sort of thing happens I should "stand in faith" and "resist the devil." The author quoted Hebrews 11:1 and said that even if the symptoms were still present, that the healing had, indeed, taken place. The author encouraged the reader to believe God, not look at the circumstances. I prayed. "Lord, I claim the healing for my cold because of what you did on the cross. I resist the devil and his lies and accept my healing of this cold, in Jesus name."

I went back to sleep with scriptures like Matthew 21:22 on my mind. Its promise was clear, "If you believe, you will receive whatever you ask for in prayer."

The next time I awoke from my nap I could hardly open my eyes. They were almost swollen shut. I could only see out a thin slit in one eye. Inside me I could sense confusion beginning to grow. Was the devil really "turning up the heat?" Or had I done something wrong? Why was I still sick? Had I missed something in the books? Why was my cold getting worse, instead of better?

I reviewed the tapes again. I had done everything that I had been told. Once again I turned my attention to heaven. "Lord, I don't know what is going on. But You said in Your Word that I have been healed by what was accomplished through Your death. You said that if I believed, I could have whatever I asked for in prayer. I know Your will is to heal me now, and I claim my healing, in Jesus name!"

My prayer continued for several more minutes. I had all the scriptures memorized and could quote them like a Harvard lawyer presenting his final argument before the judge and jury.

All the steps from the books were very clear and I was determined to get what I felt was mine. My problem was that God was not doing what the books, tapes, and scriptures said He would, and that made me upset.

I could sense the mood of my prayer time was about to change from an eloquent argument of my legal rights into an angry outburst of uncontrolled emotion. In my mind I flashed back to the many times I had believed that I had the "faith" that I needed, only to be let down with no explanation. It was like I was left alone to figure it out by myself. Angry, frustrated, burning tears rolled down my cheeks.

Through clenched teeth I told God that I had held up my end of the deal and that it was now up to Him to hold up His end. Waving furious fists heavenward I challenged the Lord, "Where is my healing? You owe it to me!" Like a small child I finished my tantrum by kicking my books, tapes and tape player off the bed onto the floor and pulled the blanket over my head.

After my tirade I collapsed in exhaustion and didn't wake up until that evening. When I did wake I couldn't see at all. My eyes were completely swollen shut.

"Hi, honey," it was Kathy. She had been reading in a chair across the room, waiting for me to wake up. "How was your day?"

"Terrible." I sneezed and my nose started to bleed.

"Here, hold this tissue over your nose. If it doesn't stop bleeding, I'll go get you a cold wash cloth. That should help."

The bleeding didn't stop until Kathy had brought the cold cloth. Rolling over, I rebuked the devil and went to sleep. Tomorrow is another day.

We had spent the weekend in Staples and I was just finishing loading our car for the return trip to Zion when I heard the tap, tap, tap, of his cane as he crossed the street. It was Merle Ford. Merle lived across the street from my folks. He was totally blind, yet he operated the vending machines at the vocational school. I didn't know him real well, but admired his courage and tenacity when it came to operating his own business.

"Hi, Merle," I called to him.

"Ah, Ken," he said with great satisfaction in his voice. "You're just the man I was looking for."

"Oh really," I jested. "What did I do now?"

"Nothing," he laughed. "The reason I came by was to tell you about the Business Enterprise Program for the Blind." My guitar case made a scraping sound as I squeezed it between two suitcases in the back of our car. "It sounds like you're busy, but can you spare a minute?"

"Sure."

"When I was young, a long time ago," he chuckled, "the future was not real bright for a blind person. It seemed like selling pencils on a street corner or making brooms were the only opportunities that were available.

"Then one day in 1936, my family received a letter telling about a program that the state of Minnesota was going to be involved in. The program would help a blind person get started in his own small business. I was eleven at the time and my family was shocked by the letter; it was like an impossible dream. Who would imagine that a blind person could actually operate a business? Anyway, I know you're involved in other things right now, but I wanted to tell you about the vending program so you knew it existed. I'd be happy to show you my business sometime. Just give me a call."

In the fall of 1974, Daystar purchased the Gardener Hotel in downtown Fargo, North Dakota. The facility was large enough to handle a live-in staff, weekly public meetings and weekend conferences.

Standing tall on the corner of Roberts Street and First Avenue, the five-story structure was a well known, much loved, city landmark. Its sale to a religious group raised some serious questions.

The ministries' lack of affiliation with a main line denomination and its unorthodox lifestyle had many long time residents of the area wondering just exactly what was going on. The "rumor mill" was busy churning out stories about "that cult group" that bought the Gardner. Some claimed that we were "Moonies" and some thought perhaps we were Hare Krishnas with hair. Still others asserted that the fifth floor was nothing but one giant mattress we used for our mandatory sex orgies!

Kathy and I continued our work at Zion Harbor but watched with interest as plans for the Gardner began to unfold. The new building would include a "tape room" for both audio and video production and reproduction. The vacated building in Moorhead was to be used as a Christian school.

We both wanted to move back to the area we called home, but we weren't sure if we would be needed there. I didn't want to get my hopes up, but each time I thought about setting up a tape room in Fargo, I couldn't help but get excited.

Then one fall day as I was finishing up editing a *Tape of the Month* master, Jon walked into the production studio and put his hand on my shoulder. "The ministry leadership has been meeting and it looks like you and Kathy are moving to Fargo. I'm gonna miss you." Then with a touch of tease in his voice, he added, "But until you leave, you belong to me! Now get that tape finished. We've got a deadline to meet!"

Two weeks later we loaded the contents of our Gremlin into the freight elevator of the Daystar-Gardner Ministry Center and moved into our room on the fifth floor. When the last box was unpacked we pooled our change and took the short walk to the Dutch Maid for ice cream!

The next morning I went downstairs for my first look at the area that was to become the Fargo home of Daystar Recordings. I would be sharing space with the business office in the area formerly occupied by the Gardner's lounge! The two areas were divided by a new wall. The wall had not yet been painted and sheet rock dust still lay on the floor. Much work needed to be done before we could even get the equipment set up.

Some of the equipment had already arrived from Daystar's ministry center in St. Louis Park, some was on order, and some was from my own personal collection. However, I still needed some cable, clips and plugs. Those I planned to buy at an electronic parts store that was only a couple blocks away.

The Gardner's location was ideal, as far as I was concerned. Everything I needed was within walking distance. When I needed guitar strings, Schmidt music was half a block away. When it was time to shop for a special occasion, Broadway was just a half block past Schmidt. If I needed electronic parts, Radio & TV Equipment was one way, Schaak Electronics, the other. The post office, banks, restaurants and even the Fargo Clinic were not that far away. It was perfect! I didn't have to depend on anyone for a ride anywhere. I could go there myself.

Walking back to the Gardner with my bag of plugs, jacks and miscellaneous plugs, the spring in my step reflected the joy that was in my heart.

I was leaving the dining room when I heard Dave's voice behind me.

"Ken, wait a minute. I have something to ask you." His voice was serious.

"I'd like you and Kathy to get some of our young staff together and form a music group."

"A music group? You mean the kind that performs in church?" I almost laughed out loud. The last group I had been in was in college playing rock 'n' roll in bars.

"No, not a performing group, a worship leading group. I'd like to try something new for our song services. Up to this point, we have had a song leader and a piano player for the music part of the meeting. That's been working great, but I think it would be a positive addition to have a group leading us in song."

"Good idea, Dave, but I'm not the one who you need." I protested. "I'm a self-taught guitar player, I don't know much about music and I know even less about getting a group together. I can think of at least two others who would do a much better job."

"You played guitar for our meetings in Moorhead, you get along well with the young staff here and I think you'll do fine. If you have any real problems, let me know and we'll see what we can do." He paused. "Give it a try, okay?"

"Alright," I said. "I'll give it a try."

"And," he continued, "to help you get a flavor of what I am talking about, I'd like you to come with us to a men's conference in Kansas City. The worship leading responsibilities will be shared by groups from Ann Arbor, Michigan and Auckland, New Zealand. We'll be leaving in a couple weeks and I think you'll enjoy it."

As he walked away, I had some serious doubts about his idea, yet at the same time I enjoyed the feeling of being believed in and trusted. His confidence in me made me want to do my best and live up to his expectations.

A few weeks later, I was sitting with five thousand other men in a large auditorium in Kansas City. I had been used to a song leader and piano player at our meetings at Zion and the Daystar-Gardner. Having a worship leading team was an exciting idea. The first music group to lead us was from a Catholic community in Ann Arbor, Michigan. I was shocked and pleased when the music started. It sounded like a complete orchestra! I could hear majestic tympani lay the foundation for the strings and brass. The choir of five thousand men rose to their feet and sang, "For you are my God! You alone are my joy!" Powerful lyrics in each of their songs pointed us straight to heaven.

The next morning the worship was led by David and Dale Garratt of Scripture in Song Ministries from Auckland, New Zealand. Using only a piano, their voices, and song lyrics taken directly from the Bible, these two worshipers brought us into His presence as the larger orchestra had done the night before.

I had never been in a group that size before where the only purpose was to sing and worship the King of Kings. I was surrounded by men with hands and hearts reaching toward heaven. Chills raced up and down my spine like lightning dancing in the summer sky. This is wonderful; it's beyond words. "Wouldn't it be great," I thought, "if I were healed, right here and now?" My mind took off with that idea so fast that I was practically tripping over the headlines: BLIND MAN HEALED! EYES OPENED IN MIRACLE HEALING! BLIND MAN SEES!

My musing was interrupted as the Garratts led us in a chorus from Psalm 97:9, "I exalt thee." When we sang the line, "You are exalted far above all gods," I halted the headlines. This moment is not about me and my needs. This moment is not about me being healed. It's about my Lord and his greatness! It's about the fellowship I can have with my God in worship.

I set all my questions and confusions aside and was left with only one thing: the joy in my heart that I was in His presence and that I, along with the other men, had the honor and thrill of making His heart glad!

It was coffee break and I left the tape room to get a doughnut and a glass of milk for a quick snack.

"Hey, Ken. Can I talk to you for a minute?" The voice belonged to Elmer Johnson. Elmer was a retired pastor who was on staff with us. He and his wife Dorothy had been caring for a young autistic girl and I knew that they had wrestled with the issue of divine healing, too.

"Sure, Elmer. What's up?"

We sat down in a booth in the corner of the dining room.

"Ken, I've been thinking about you lately. I've been thinking about your desire to be healed." Elmer had my full attention. This was a subject that I was happy to talk about at any time.

I knew from his experience as a pastor and long life as a Christian, that he had lived through some things that I had not. After a short pause, he continued.

"I'm wondering, Ken, if God isn't more interested in your getting to know Him better, than He is in healing you."

I thanked him for sharing his thoughts with me. But something inside of me still wanted my miracle.

Having been in the ministry for several years, Kathy and I had developed a system for going through buffet lines. We each took a plate and Kathy, walking ahead of me, would tell me what was on the table. When it came to rolls, toast, cookies or anything I could easily pick up, I would serve myself. But when it came to spaghetti, salad or mashed potatoes, she would put it on my plate. This system kept the line moving quickly and also kept the serving table clean! One day the potato soup was particularly good so I decided to return for a second bowl.

"Do you need my help?" Kathy asked.

"I don't think so. I remember where the soup kettle is, thanks."

At the serving table I located the rounded kettle that I assumed had the soup in it and filled my bowl and returned to the table. I set the bowl next to my milk and continued eating my other food when I noticed the table conversation had ceased. All that remained was an awkward silence. Then came that uncomfortable feeling. You know the one: everyone is staring at you? Well, I felt like everyone at the table was staring at me.

Then Kathy leaned over and whispered in my ear, "Honey, what did you plan to do with that bowl of gravy?"

Chapter 12

Do You See What I Hear?

Sunny summer days were made for canoeing on the Crow Wing River. The gentle nudge of the waves against the canoe, the mysterious call of the loon and the soft splash of the mud turtle as it slips from its sun-warmed rock into the silky water--all contribute to the therapeutic value of a quiet journey downstream.

Kathy and I were in Staples over the weekend and learned that my brother Jon's girlfriend Debbie was in town. Since the weatherman was forecasting a cloudless sky and temperatures in the mid eighties, we decided to invite them on a short canoe trip. The route we chose was a familiar one—from Bullard's Bluff to my folks' place by McGivern Park. The trip would be a two-to-three-hour float.

Jon and Debbie arrived that morning and were in the midst of a fun loving and rather spirited conversation. Debbie is deaf so Jon was signing and moving his lips to present his side of the story. Debbie, in turn, was speaking and gesturing broadly to get her point across. I couldn't see the signs, so I only caught half of what was being said. I think it had something to do with which side of the canoe you should paddle on if you want the canoe to go to the right.

When Dad returned from town, he was going to give us a ride to Bullard's Bluff. While we were waiting, we loaded two of his war-horse canoes into the back of Old Red, his faithful pickup. Next came the coolers full of munchies and we were ready to go.

We followed the bumpy, dusty back roads that brought us to Bullard's Bluff. Jon and I sat in the back to make sure the coolers and canoes didn't bounce out of the rickety old truck. Dad, Kathy and Debbie rode in the cab. When we arrived at our destination, we pulled the canoes from the pickup and slid them down the slippery bank into the river.

Jon and Debbie rode in the first canoe. Jon sat in the back to rudder and Debbie sat in the front. Each time he wanted to communicate with her he would thump his paddle against the side of the canoe. When Debbie felt the vibrations, she would turn around and read his lips. He used that method to call her attention to a deer camouflaged by the forest or a blue heron that was almost hidden in a shady bayou.

Once on the river, time seemed to stand still. We let our canoes drift with the current--no schedules to meet, no ringing of phones. It was just us, a free afternoon and the quiet strength of the river.

Warm sunshine fell on my back as I dangled my feet outside the canoe in the refreshing water. Off in the distance birds sang and called to one another. Up close, the waves lapped against the canoe. Now and then I'd hear the crackling of twigs breaking under the cautious steps of deer that had come down to the river to get a drink. Taking a deep breath, I filled my lungs with the moist aroma of the forest.

Occasionally our canoes would scrape bottom when we got too close to a sandbar. Other times we would round a bend to find someone fishing in one of the river's many fishing holes.

It seemed as if we had only been on the river for a short time when we started to recognize the landmarks that told us we were nearing our destination. The first was the mouth of the Leaf River where it empties into the Crow Wing; next came the houses that are upstream from where my parents live.

When we were getting close to our landing, I started to power paddle so our canoe would cut across the current and plant us firmly on the river bank.

Jon and Debbie had reached the shore before Kathy and me. He had already pulled the canoe onto the bank, and Debbie had gone into the house to change into some dry clothes before supper.

On her way through the kitchen she stopped and commented to Mom, "I don't think I'd like to be blind. Ken missed so much on the river today. He couldn't see the blue water, the birds flying in the sky or even the turtle on the rock."

A few minutes later I entered the kitchen and commented to Mom, "I don't think I'd like to be deaf. Debbie missed so much on the river today. She couldn't hear the water lapping at the side of the canoes, the chirping of the birds or even the soft splash of the turtle when it fell off it's rock."

After one of our Wednesday evening services, I overheard a couple students talking about the new External Studies program at Moorhead State. Curious, I stopped and joined in the conversation. They told me that it was designed for non-traditional students. The program made it possible to receive college credit for previous work experience. They asked me if I was thinking of returning to school.

The thought had not entered my mind since Kathy and I had joined Daystar. As far as I was concerned, I didn't really need to finish my degree. I was already employed in my field. And since I had no intention of leaving Daystar, I didn't really see a need for a degree in my future, either.

Nevertheless, this news started me thinking about returning to Moorhead State. In some ways, it did bother me that I had not finished my degree. If, by being in this program, I could reduce the amount of time I needed to spend in the classroom and receive enough credits to graduate in one year, it might be worth it.

The next day I contacted Audrey Jones, director of the External Studies Department. I explained my situation to her and she thought that I would fit into the program very well. It would involve writing papers, getting letters from past and present work supervisors, department chairmen signatures and detailed descriptions of work duties. Between upper level courses taken as independent study, credit from prior work experience and a couple classes each quarter, it looked like I could finish in one year. So in the fall of 1976, I became a college student once again.

With Kathy's help, I wrestled through what seemed like reams of forms so that I could receive credit for my work in setting up the audio-video tape ministry at the hotel. The final result of that project was an operating manual that explained how everything was hooked together and the procedures to go through to make it all run as one.

To help fulfill my humanities requirement, I took a psychology course titled *Personality*. Part of our final grade would be based on a paper that we were to write about ourselves, a sort of auto-biography. Our instructor said he was not so much interested in personal data, but he wanted to know about three factors that contributed to making each of us the person we were today. It was to include footnotes and a bibliography. The three areas I chose to write on were: the influence my parents had on me, my eyesight, and my relationship with God. I titled my paper, "The Making of Me".

It was easy writing about my parents, and my God, but when I started writing about my eyesight, and how it had affected my life, my writing slowed, considerably. I had spent most of my life trying to ignore my blindness. Now in this paper, I had to focus on it and to write about its effects.

During that same time, our study group at the hotel was reading the book, Don't Waste Your Sorrows, which discussed the role of suffering in the life of a Believer. I had also come across a poem that Barry McGuire had put to music.

I walked a mile with pleasure
She chattered all the way.
But left me none the wiser
For all she had to say
I walked a mile with sorrow
Never a word said she
But oh, the things I learned from her
When sorrow walked with me.

The books I used in my paper talked about how adversity and life's challenges can actually help in the maturing process. "My eyesight is the source of much emotion," I wrote. "At times I am angered by it because I want to do certain things, but can't. One thing that I have learned is that you can't always have what you want."

I was stuck between two truths. On one hand, it was clear that we serve a God of love and compassion. On the other hand, I heard other voices saying that personal wisdom and maturity can only be grown in "the valley".

Several of us graduated from college that spring. To help celebrate, the Daystar-Gardner had a reception in the Colonial Room of the hotel. Many friends and relatives attended the event, including my folks. They drove over from Staples to spend the afternoon.

The graduates and their guests waited in the lobby while the last minute preparations were completed. When the doors were opened and we walked across the lobby toward the dining room, I felt my dad's hand on my shoulder, "I'm proud of you, son." I always knew he was. But his words made me smile.

Chapter 13

Outlaws and Angels

The muffled sound of traffic on Roberts Street drifted through our open window. Kathy and I were just about to watch the ten o'clock news when the phone rang.

"Ken? They're gonna kill me! You gotta help me!" The voice was familiar and in a panic. I'll call him Jake.

The first time I met Jake was years ago at the Encounter House where he had become a Christian. Then a couple years later, I heard he had given up on Christianity, and then, a couple years after that, he was a Christian again.

Small in stature, he could explode with demon power at the slightest provocation. While he was not a member, he did spend a good deal of time with a local outlaw biker club. Stories about him fighting men twice his size were common. Each of those stories ended with Jake as the victor.

I spoke calmly into the receiver. "Kill you? What do you mean?" I hoped it was a joke.

"They put a contract out on me and they are going to kill me! I need your help!" This wasn't a joke. The stress in his voice said it was true.

"Okay, wait a minute. Calm down. Let's start from the beginning. Who wants to kill you?"

"Some bikers."

"Bikers? Why do they want to kill you?"

"Because of the pictures…." He grew quiet.

"What pictures?"

"The pictures I took of this biker's girlfriend." He paused for a moment. "I was walking back to my apartment from downtown when I spotted this girl in her back yard sunbathing. I stopped and struck up a conversation with her and asked if I could take a few Polaroids. She said I could so I took a few outside and then we went inside to take some more. After I ran out of film, she said she wanted me to give her the pictures. I said they were mine and left. Then I found out that her boyfriend put a contract out on me. Ken, you are the only one who can help me. What should I do?"

The *hero* inside me rose to the occasion. Yes, I was sure we could solve his problem quite easily.

"First off, I assume you are aware that taking those pictures was a poor idea. In fact, it was a terrible idea." I couldn't resist the opportunity to pass on a little advice to my captive audience. "You shouldn't have even stopped when you saw her. You should have looked the other way and kept on walking. I think it was Billy Graham who once said, 'You can't keep a bird from flying over your head, but you can keep it from building a nest in your hair.'"

"Yes, yes, I know you're right, but what do I do now?"

"You need to return those pictures and get your contract cancelled." I felt like Eliot Ness in an episode of the Untouchables! "Do you think they would call it off if you gave them the pictures?"

"Maybe, yeah, probably."

"Good. Then let's pray for the Lord's blessing as you go."

"Wait," he interrupted. "Will you go with me? I would feel better if you were there."

I paused a moment. How could I refuse help to someone in trouble? It seemed to me that it would be a simple task to return the pictures and cancel the contract. How difficult could that be?

"Okay, Jake, I'll go with you."

"Thank you! I'll come by the hotel and we can go together. I'm on my way."

Jake didn't have a car, but he lived within walking distance of the hotel.

Hanging up the phone, I told Kathy what I was going to do. "Can you find a couple folks who will pray for us while we are gone?"

I went downstairs and arrived in the lobby only a few minutes before Jake. Feeling very confident that everything would work out fine, the two of us left the hotel on foot.

We crossed First Avenue and headed north past the courthouse. As we

114

walked, I took the opportunity to talk to Jake about his spiritual life. I told him he was going to continue to get himself into trouble if he didn't change his ways. He listened politely as I lectured, but I could sense he was not hearing a word I said. He was tense, distracted by something unseen. Every time a car passed us he acted jumpy--perhaps paranoid.

Our route led us away from the noise of downtown to the quiet of an older neighborhood. Huge elm and maple trees lined the boulevard to my left. Large two and three story houses were set back from the sidewalk on our right. All the houses were dark. Everyone must have gone to bed.

Then the quiet of the neighborhood was broken by squealing tires. A car was speeding in our direction from somewhere behind us. Its headlights cast weird shadows on the ground in front of us. When it was beside us, it slowed to a crawl. In a low whisper he said, "Don't look, don't stop, just keep walking."

Suddenly I was not as confident as I had been just moments before. An icy chill ran down the back of my neck. Then without warning, the accelerator was slammed into the floor boards and the car sped away leaving us in a cloud of exhaust fumes. What had I gotten myself into?

Moments later, Jake stopped in front of a large two-story house. "Here it is. They live in the upstairs apartment." The tone of his voice was sober. "I don't see any light in the windows. No one's here. Let's go."

"Now wait a minute, Jake. Not so fast. We've come this far, we can't just leave!" I was anxious to get this job done and get back to the security of the hotel.

We followed the drive way to the rear entrance, opened the screen door and stepped inside. My nose was assaulted by the stench of rancid cooking oil and stale cigarette smoke. Under the floor boards, the porch must've doubled as a mouse grave yard. Straight ahead of us was the door that led to the ground floor apartment and to its left was the staircase that led to the second floor.

"Let's go." Jake whispered, and then waited. "Maybe you should go first."

I looked at the narrow, dingy stairway. It was probably only two feet wide and poorly lit. It reminded me of something out of an old horror movie. I wasn't sure I wanted to see who, or what was waiting for us at the top.

With each step I took the wooden stairs creaked. Jake was right behind me. The closer we got to the top the more insecure I became. This was not a game, or a fairy tale where everyone is guaranteed to live "happily ever after." This was really happening--and it was happening to me.

When we reached the third step from the top, Jake tapped me on the shoulder as if to say, "Stop, we're close enough." There was no landing at the top of the stairs, just the apartment door. Jake reached out his hand and knocked. An angry male voice growled from inside.

"Who is it?"

"It's Jake. I want to give the pictures back."

From inside the apartment, heavy boot steps cross the floor. After a brief pause, the door swung open. The man could have been a twelve-foot giant. His enormous frame held the dim light in the apartment prisoner, leaving Jake and me in the dark.

"Who's he?" The man demanded. I assumed he was referring to me.

"His name is Ken. He's a friend. Where is Lori? I want to give the pictures back."

"She ain't here. Give 'em to me." The big man's voice was insistent.

"Not a chance." Jake's voice took on an angry tone. "I'll only give them to Lori!"

"What's the matter? Don't you trust me?"

"I'll only give 'em to Lori." Jake's voice was firm.

From inside the apartment another man's voice bellowed, "What's the problem?"

"It's Jake. He's got Lori's pictures."

"If he won't trust us with 'em, tell him to come in and call her."

The big man stepped aside and Jake and I went into the apartment. It reeked of stale cigarette smoke and body odor. I guessed that we were now in the kitchen. Out of the corner of my eye I could see several dark circles on the wall near the door. They were probably frying pans or skillets. A dark people-shape at the table, I assumed, was the other man who had spoken.

Jake went across the room to the phone and began to dial. Following him into the unfriendly apartment, I began to seriously question my decision to come with him. It had seemed like it was the right thing to do when I was back at the hotel, but at that moment, I wasn't so sure.

My thoughts were interrupted when the big man slammed the door behind us. It sounded like it was made of iron, not hollow pine. Then he stood by the closed door like a vicious guard dog blocking the only exit from the apartment.

Standing to my left, Jake was not getting an answer to his phone calls. With

116

each spin of the rotary dial I could feel his anger grow. To my right, the big man was getting more hostile, too. "Just leave the pictures here. I'll see that she gets 'em."

"I'll give 'em to Lori and nobody else," Jake snapped back as he furiously spun the dial.

The tension between these two men was at a critical level. It felt like there could be a fight at any time— and there I stood—right between them. I started to shake like a one-hundred-fifteen-pound bowl of Jell-O and I prayed as I had never prayed before.

Jake dialed the phone once more and finally got an answer. By this time, the big man was pacing back and forth in front of the door. He had something in his hand and was banging it on the skillet shapes that hung on the wall. I couldn't see what it was but the low pitched "thuds" told me that whatever it was, it was hard and heavy.

"Lori says I'm supposed to leave the pictures with you." Jake was addressing the big man who was hitting the skillet shapes with more force than before.

Then the big man turned in our direction and spoke in a hoarse whisper. "Why'd you do it?"

"Look, I talked to Lori. She said I should leave them with you. Here are the pictures." Jake pulled something from his pocket and held it out for the big man.

"I don't mean the pictures!" The big man raised his voice, almost shouting, "I mean why'd you have to hit her? Why'd you have to beat her up?"

My search for the nearest fire exit stopped in mid-scan. What did he just say? I looked in Jake's direction as if to say, "What is this guy talking about? Who got hit? Who got beat up? What's going on here? I thought we came here to give back some pictures. You didn't say anything about anyone getting beat up!" Any hope for a peaceful solution to this problem now lay in shambles at my feet.

I could imagine Jake bristle and glare at the big man. The growing hostility between the two told me that these mighty lions were about to rumble and I was standing between them with no where to go.

The fierce tension in the room was suddenly broken when we heard the screen door at the bottom of the stairs bang closed, followed by the sound of heavy boots climbing the creaky steps. Time stood still as we waited for the new comers to reach the apartment. Would they be friend or foe? Four people shapes entered through the door. Soon, I thought, I'll find out if it's true that Saint Peter greets everyone at the Pearly Gates.

"Okay everybody, calm down. What's going on here?"

The man's voice was commanding and full of authority. Then he walked right up to me. He was a member of the Fargo Police Department.

"Who are you?" he demanded. I suspect my white pants, matching face and sweat drenched plaid polyester short sleeve shirt gave him the impression that I was not a regular guest at that apartment.

"K—K—Ken M—M—Miller," I stuttered. "I'm from the Daystar-Gardner Ministry Center."

Once again the screen door banged closed and heavy boots were heard on the stairs. Another two figures entered the room. This time the new arrivals were some of Lori's outlaw biker friends and they were not happy to see the police. Some harsh words were spoken and soon other officers came up the stairs into the crowded apartment.

"Mr. Miller, would you follow me downstairs to my car? I have some questions to ask you."

"No problem," my voice cracked. "Lead the way!" We walked out of the house and were instantly bathed in a sea of bright light.

On the way down the drive way to his car, looking around me, I counted seven flashing lights. I guess that meant that there were seven squad cars at the scene. All around me I could hear the crackle of police radios and the sound of officers talking.

Once inside his car, I started to relax and feel safe again. I answered all of his questions as best I could. He gave me a ride back to the hotel and suggested I be more selective about the company I keep.

Safe, back in my room, I collapsed in our easy chair and told Kathy about my evening adventure.

"Were you able to find someone to pray with you?" I asked.

"Yes, Barb and Mary."

"What did you pray for?"

"We prayed God would send angels to protect you."

"He certainly did. But tonight," I smiled as I thought about the evening. "They left their robes behind and wore uniforms."

Chapter 14

My American Dream

I finished transferring some dates from a typewritten sheet to our music calendar when I was overcome with a deep sense of satisfaction and pride. Once again, the calendar was full. Pushing my chair away from the desk, I leaned back and thought about my life and how fulfilled I felt. Many things had changed in the last five years since we drove that little purple Gremlin down that narrow back road to the green house at Zion Harbor.

Our musical travels had taken us from Philadelphia to San Diego, from Prince Albert, Saskatchewan, to Brownsville, Texas, and from Winnipeg, Canada to Kailua Kona, Hawaii, and countless places in between. We had been privileged to work with some very talented musicians and were prepared to offer music ministry in a variety of settings, from performance to leading worship.

My work in the tape room was finished. It could operate without me. The manual I had developed when I returned to Moorhead State was left in the control room and contained everything anyone needed to know about its operation. Several staff members were trained on the equipment so that we could rotate responsibilities during weekend conferences.

Smiling, I remembered, with Lyle Amundson's encouragement, studying for my ham radio license. Along with Don, Gerald, Ed, Mark and several others, we established radio stations at several of the Daystar Ministry centers and sent messages across the country to staff members and to various overseas missionaries.

Recently, Kathy and I had become a part of the leadership team that served the functional and spiritual needs of the Daystar-Gardner community. I was proud of the contributions that I had made to that ministry.

Like a locomotive speeding across the plains, I had purpose, direction and fulfillment. Behind me I was pulling a long train of railroad cars. Each one was marked with its own name: "music ministry", "tape room", "Daystar" and "community living". Everything was functioning smoothly and in an orderly manner.

From my seat in the engine I could survey the land around me and feel the strength of the steel beneath me. Then, racing across a trestle, that powerful locomotive was violently derailed, as if from an earthquake, and thrown from the tracks leaving smashed cars scattered like spilled match sticks on the canyon floor.

Was it dynamite? Was it sabotage from an unseen enemy? Was it a bomb? Was it a head-on collision with another train? No, it was none of the above. The train toppled off the trestle because of a seven-pound baby boy named Michael. He reached out to me with that tiny little hand and grabbed my heart and wouldn't let go! I was a father! I had a son! We were a family!

I turned my gaze from him long enough to take a quick look at the canyon floor. Through the cloud of dust I could see cars strewn everywhere, their twisted frames mangled beyond recognition. The two cars that sustained the most damage read "Daystar" and "community living". The great train that I had been pulling was wrecked and like Humpty Dumpty, it could not be put back together again.

My place in the ministry, that "perfect fit", was now strangely uncomfortable. The "new father" in me was in contact with a whole new set of priorities and that comfortable pair of blue jeans I loved so much had suddenly turned into a stifling straight jacket. I needed to provide for my new family. I needed to bring home the bacon. It was time for me to take hold of my piece of the American dream.

Luther Matsen's name was at the top of my new to-do list. He had been director of the Daystar-Gardner for the past two years and he needed to know my plan.

"Luther," I began, "I don't know how to say this, so I'm just going to say it. I need to leave community and live on my own for a season. I'm not sure if this means I'll never live in community again, but right now I need to be on my own. Something inside me needs to be able to say that I did it myself."

After a long pause, he spoke. "I can see that your mind is made up. Of course, I'd like you to stay, but I do hear what you are saying. I must also say that we will miss you."

Safety and security surrounded me in the ministry. I knew what I needed to do and when and where to do it. Getting around the building and downtown Fargo had become second nature. But now things were different. Standing in front of me was a world of unknowns.

The first thing I'd need to do upon leaving Daystar was to get a job. Jon Lyle had been my work supervisor at Zion Harbor and Jack Trump at the Gardner. Each wrote a glowing letter of recommendation to go with my resumé. It would have been fun to work with the guy they described.

With my letters and an updated resumé in hand, my search began immediately by visiting local radio and TV stations. Unknown to me at that time, the job market was flooded by people with my degree and experience. To make matters worse, many radio and TV stations were laying people off, not hiring. Typically, the secretary at the front desk would tell me to put my resumé in the pile with the others.

Since it seemed the mass communications area was closed, I started to broaden my search. Dad called some people he knew in the Twin Cities area. They didn't have anything at that time, but said try again later. Northwestern Bell was hiring so I walked the few blocks to their offices to take one of their tests; no interview followed.

As days turned into weeks, I became more and more discouraged about finding work. Finally, I called my SSB counselor, Lowell Lysaker, and complained about my frustrations in job hunting.

"Have you ever thought of working for yourself?" He asked.

Working for myself? The concept had never entered my mind. All my educational energy had been spent on developing skills to be a good employee. I had never, in my wildest dreams, thought of working for myself.

"No," I told him, "I never have, but I am definitely interested!"

"The state of Minnesota has a program that gives persons, who are blind or legally blind, the opportunity to operate their own small businesses."

"What types of businesses?"

"Snack bars, cafeterias, vending break rooms and vending routes. Our training program will teach you everything you need to know from equipment repair and maintenance to bookkeeping and public relations. The first part of the training experience is in the classroom, the second is on the job with a blind vendor who is already in business. Income from these enterprises is respectable. Does that sound like something you would like to do?"

Remembering Merle Ford and his vending machine business, I smiled, "Does it ever!"

"Then I will set up an appointment for you with our training supervisor, Tom Nicklawske."

Days later, descending the stairs at 1745 University Avenue in St. Paul, my lungs were filled with the aroma of freshly-brewed coffee and my mind with freshly-brewed apprehension. Today, I would have my interview with Mr. Tom Nicklawske. We'd meet in what Mr. Lysaker called the "training stand". It seemed like a small coffee shop to me, except the proprietor, Janice Coleman, was blind.

Sitting at a booth around the corner, away from the till, I listened to the background music and occasional chat from customers making their purchases. Then, my senses came to attention when a friendly, but professional voice asked, "Are you Ken Miller?"

"Yes, I am."

We went over my background and work experience and then turned to program expectations.

Several days later, our phone rang.

"Ken." It was Mr. Lysaker. "I spoke with Mr. Nicklawske this morning. Your interview went very well. I know you want to start as soon as possible, but the earliest date we could find to begin your training is in mid-June."

"Mid-June!" I protested. "This is May 5th!"

"I know it seems a long way off. But Mr. Nicklawske told me that his schedule is full right now and that's the earliest starting date he has available. He currently has two students in the training program and they won't be finished for six weeks or so."

"Okay," I said, a bit disappointed that I couldn't start sooner.

"Mr. Nicklawske also asked me if you use a cane. I told him you did not and he told me that, before you begin as a student in the Business Enterprise

Program, you should learn how to use one."

"A cane? I've never used one in my life. Why should I start now?"

"For one thing, it will help identify you to others as a person who is visually impaired. You will find that identification very helpful when you are in the Twin Cities. For instance, as part of your training experience, you will be working with several blind vendors who already have their own businesses. Those businesses are located all over the metro area and you will need to use the bus system to go from place to place. Sometimes it will be necessary to transfer from one bus to another. If the driver sees you standing at the stop with a white cane, he or she will tell you the bus number when the bus door opens."

"I don't know anything about canes. Can you show me how to use one?"

"I am not an expert, but I can show you enough to get started."

The next day I stood in Mr. Lysaker's office and he handed me a collapsible white cane. It was very light weight, composed of six pieces of aluminum tubing with a long elastic cord that ran through the center of each tube. The ends of each tube were tapered to fit snugly into each other. Once all the tubes were hooked together they made a cane that, when stood straight up, reached from the floor to just under my shoulder. When not in use, it could be folded up and set out of the way, or stuck into my back pocket.

Having lived my entire life without one, the cane felt clumsy in my hand. We started walking down the hallway and he told me that the tip of the cane would give me feedback as to what was ahead of me. As I swung the cane in a two-to-three-foot arch in front of me, I could feel the smoothness of the hallway floor followed by the friction created by the rug at the top of the stairs. When I reached the first step, I could feel the cane drop off the edge.

"You probably don't need to use your cane on the steps," he said. "Take hold of the railing with one hand and hold your cane in the other."

We walked up and down the hallway a few more times before returning to his office.

"I've made an appointment for you at the Minneapolis Society for the Blind. They will teach you how to use the bus system and answer any questions you may have about getting around the cities. Here is the address and time." He handed me a piece of paper that I put into my shirt pocket. Then a flash of movement told me he had extended his hand. "I know you are going to make a fine operator in this program. Let me know if you need anything." I shook his hand and left the office. Folding up the white cane and putting it in my back pocket, I hopped on my bike and rode back to the Daystar-Gardner.

Awkward weeks passed as we made arrangements to leave the Daystar-Gardner. Conversation with fellow staff members was uncomfortable. Plans were being made for next fall's conference schedule and everyone knew that Ken and Kathy would not be there.

The first place we called home in the Twin Cities was on 42nd and Pillsbury in south Minneapolis, just a few blocks from Lake Harriet. Sunshine and the mid-June temperature sent us to the lake right after a quick bite to eat. We sat in the cool sand as Michael played with his shovel and pail.

Even though I was surrounded by the sounds of the city, my mind was busy with the next day's activities. Kathy was going to drop me off at the MSB offices where I was going to learn how to use the bus system. My schooling in the BEP began in two days and using the bus was a must. After learning the ropes I'd take a bus home rather than call Kathy.

Leaving our car, I tightened the grip I had on my cane. I was more excited than I was nervous. A new door was about to open for me: a transportation door! Once I understood the ins-and-outs of bus riding, I could go almost anywhere by myself. Knowledge of the bus system and the white cane in my hand would be my personal declaration of independence.

I was taken to an office upstairs where a young man told me the basic rules of bus riding. He covered everything from calling the MTC for route information, to determining which corner of the intersection I should stand on to meet my bus. We looked at some large print maps and intersection diagrams to help me get a better picture of where the buses stopped. When I felt confident that I knew how it all worked, he handed me a phone.

"Do you want to give it a try?"

"Yes," I said, "I believe I do."

Filling the blank page of typewriter paper with large letters, I scrawled two addresses—where I was and where I wanted to go, and dialed the number for route information. The lines were busy, but eventually, my call was answered.

The voice at the other end of the line told me I could catch a bus at Franklin and Lyndale, which was right outside the MSB front door! She then gave me the rest of the information I needed and I was set. Thanking the young man for his help, I headed down the stairs to await my bus.

Standing outside MSB waiting for the bus, I let a goofy grin stretch across my face. This was it! I was free! Soon I'd exit the bus, hurry to the house, burst through the door and yell, "Honey, I'm home!"

Then my quiet revelry was interrupted by her voice.

"Are you waiting for a bus young man?" The voice belonged to an elderly lady.

"Yes, I am."

"Well then, we better get you across the street right away so you don't miss it!" Clamping my elbow with the vice at the end of her arm, she dragged me into the street before I could utter a single word of protest.

"But, ma'am..."

"We don't want you to miss your bus!"

"But, ma'am..."

"Just a few more steps and we'll be at your corner."

I could not get free of her grip. She was determined to get me to the other side of the street so that I wouldn't miss my bus.

"Now you just hang on for a couple more steps. Step up for the curb! There we go," she said with satisfaction, "safe and sound. Can you make it from here?"

I didn't know what to say. "Umm...yes, ma'am. Thank you, ma'am."

She turned and headed in the other direction, probably feeling quite good about having helped a blind guy to cross the road.

Waiting for the light to change, the grin returned. Life is good. I crossed the street and took my position.

Moments later I heard the rumble of a diesel engine and the squeal of brakes as a bus pulled up in front of me. The driver called out the number and I boarded. I asked him if he would call out 42nd when we reached my stop and then I took a seat.

Knowing the bus ride was going to take some time, I folded my cane and held it on my lap. Good feelings flooded my entire being. It was hard to believe that I was in the middle of Minneapolis, on a bus, by myself, headed home. Up to that point in my life, I had never tasted such a level of independence, and it tasted real good!

Chapter 15

Takin' Care of Business

Entering the BEP training program was like entering a whole new world. All my life I had been adapting to sighted-world education, but this training program, it seemed, had been designed especially for me. No longer in a class of thirty trying to learn by listening to the instructor and wishing I could see what he was writing on the blackboard, I was in a class of two where learning was hands-on.

The vending machine training area had a large number of machines that were ready for students to study. When we worked on a machine, Tom moved two of the same type close together and then would instruct us as we would "look" at the equipment. It seemed like the number of machines to learn was endless: canned pop, cup pop, pastry, snack, coffee, hot food and cold food. We would be learning each of these machines, inside and out.

We learned about each new piece of vending equipment the same way. First, Tom had us examine the outside of the front door, taking note of where the coin insert, coin return, selection buttons and delivery door were located. Then we'd move to the inside of the door and then the inside of the machine itself. Slowly, methodically, step-by-step, we learned how each one worked.

He also taught us how to remove some of the parts, like coin acceptors, changers, valves, pumps and canisters. Once out of the machine, they could be placed on a work bench and taken apart for repair. The only part of the machine he did not show us on our machine tours was the cash box. He said that, somehow, operators always knew where that was.

The door to the coffee machine was standing wide open as I glared into the gloomy interior. My busy hands told me it looked like a jumble of hoses, wires, little plastic bowls and who-knows-what. Sighing deeply, I continued my exploring.

"What's that?" I heard Roger's voice from his coffee machine that was next to mine. Roger was my classmate.

"What a mess. Learning the inside of this machine is not going to be easy," I said.

"Nah," said Roger confidently. "Learning this machine will be a piece of cake!"

"I hope you're right," I mumbled as I stuck my head back into the machine.

"Of course he's right." I heard Tom's voice from behind me. "Ken, don't use your eyes when you learn this equipment. Learn to identify things by touch. It may surprise you, but you'll find that you'll be able to do things faster if you don't look. And when you troubleshoot a problem, learn to listen. Listening will tell you things you couldn't see, even if you could see."

That was the first time I had ever been told not to use my eyes. I had to adjust my whole way of thinking. Instead of being a partially-blind man in a sighted world, I was now a partially-sighted man in a blind world.

We were getting close to finishing our third week of study on the model 614 coffee machine when Tom told us that he would be gone for a couple of days.

"I brought you boys a little something to work on while I'm gone," he said with mischief in his voice.

"Oh boy," we each responded with phony enthusiasm. "What could it be?"

"Actually, there are two 'little somethings'. One for each of you. Follow me."

We followed Tom around the corner to the area where we worked on the machines. "We pulled two coffee machines from a machine shop today and I'd like you guys to clean them up while I am gone."

"What do you mean, clean them up?" I asked.

"I want you to remove all the dry ingredients canisters, mixing bowls, whippers, hoses, the heat exchanger, the cup well, the brewer, all the product valves and buckets. Then I want you to clean the inside of the machine and all the parts you removed. Next, I want you to take the brewer and valves apart and replace all the seals, gaskets, heart valve in the brewer barrel, and valve seats. After that, I want you to take all the dry ingredients' canisters apart and clean their insides. Finally, I want you to remove the hoses that run from the water inlet valve to the heat exchanger and the one that runs from the heat exchanger to the water feeder cup and clean them with a wire brush.

"Yes," Roger chimed in. "How long did you say you were going to be gone?"

"Two days and the weekend. I'll see you on Monday."

We turned to face our machines. The doors were open with tables sitting beside each one so we would have a place to put the parts from the inside. Tom had left us tools on the tables.

Roger and I attacked those machines like a couple of nutty Ninjas. Two days is not a lot of time, especially if something went wrong.

But by Friday afternoon, our task was complete. We had finished with both machines and had even made ourselves some coffee to make sure they worked. Actually, the coffee was not real coffee. In school we did not use grounds, nor was the heater plugged in. A machine that uses cold water does not burn as you learn.

Monday morning rolled around and Roger and I walked into the area where our machines were waiting. We were wearing triumphant grins.

"Good morning, boys." Tom was already there waiting for us. "How about making me a nice cup of coffee?"

"It would be our pleasure!" We pushed the buttons that would set the machines in motion. Instantly, there was water spraying everywhere!

Roger and I dove inside those machines trying to locate the source of the spray. We couldn't understand it. We had run them Friday before we left for the weekend and they had worked just fine.

The water seemed to be coming from the brewer so I removed the cover and reached inside. Sure enough, the hose that ran from the brewer to the coffee mixing bowl was not attached. Instead of running into the mixing bowl and then to the cup, the water had sprayed all over the inside of the machine!

"Tom," Roger asked, with just a touch of suspicion in his voice, "you wouldn't know anything about these disconnected hoses by any chance?"

"No, of course not," was Tom's poorly disguised denial. "It is important, however, that you learn how to trouble shoot and repair these machines yourself. You could end up with a business in northern Minnesota and have to work on it alone. You won't be able to call us to fix it for you."

The coin mechanisms in snack and candy machines could double as boat anchors. The area where prices are set resembles a miniature, old fashioned telephone switchboard. To set the prices, ten tiny wires plug into a horizontal row of holes above the pricing wheel. Each wire has its own color or pattern and must be placed in a certain order with the others for the mechanism to work properly.

"If you move one wire at a time," Tom said, "you shouldn't have a problem setting the prices."

"What if I'm working on a machine and a wire comes loose?" I interrupted.

"Ask someone nearby if they would tell you the color of the wire. Once you know its color, you can figure out where it goes. If you can demonstrate your competence with the equipment, most folks would be happy to tell you the color. On the other hand, if you were to say to someone, 'This is broken. Will you fix it?' you probably won't make a good impression. Remember, like it or not, your actions are being watched by the public and your customers. That impression needs to be a positive one."

In early September, we moved from Minneapolis to an apartment in St. Paul. Basically, all that meant was that after school, to get home, I'd catch an east-bound 16A rather than one that was west bound.

Late one afternoon I stepped off the bus at Rice and Wheelock and started across the parking lot to our apartment building. Walking passed Kentucky Fried Chicken, my nose filled with ideas for supper and my soul filled with pride. I felt like that little kid on the TV commercial who declares, "Look ma, I can do it myself."

Snow flakes were falling from the early morning sky and landing gently on my face. I was standing on the street corner waiting for the bus that would take me to the Ramsey County Welfare building on East Kellogg Boulevard. I had been working for Joe Lazarich in the cafeteria there for almost two weeks. At the end of this week, my training experience would be complete and the next thing to do would be to wait for a business to become available.

Joe's business was primarily food service, but he also operated several vending machines in other parts of the building. I found myself drawn more to those vending machines than the cafeteria.

Counting cans of peas in the store room, I heard Joe call my name from the office. "Ken, the phone is for you. You can use the one on the wall by the door."

"Ken?"

"Yes."

"This is Chuk Hamilton, BEP supervisor. We have an opening in the program at the Ah-Gwah-Ching nursing home near Walker. We have gone through the seniority list of current vendors and also the eligibility list and no one has taken the business. You are almost finished training and I wonder if you would be interested in seeing it."

"What kind of business is it?"

"It's an all-vending machine business but there is one part-time employee who prepares sandwiches and salads for the food vending machines…."

"Vending machines?" I interrupted. "How many?"

"Eight and one dollar-changer in the employee break room and four in the residents' lounge across the hall."

"I'll take it!" I said.

"Without even looking at it?"

"Umm," I paused, "I better look at it. But if it has vending machines, I'm sure I'll like it."

"Excellent," he said. "Can we go look at it tomorrow?"

"Absolutely."

Hanging up the phone, my heart rate increased and a silly smile stretched across my face. This was the moment I had been waiting for: I was going to be working in my own business and supporting my family! And to make things even better, it included vending machines!

Two weeks later we were almost finished counting the inventory I would be assuming as manager of the "Vend-A-Bar," when a customer walked up to the coffee machine and inserted a coin. The machine performed perfectly, pouring the freshly brewed java into the waiting cup. As the customer walked to her table for her afternoon break, Chuk spoke softly, "Ken, you just made your first quarter."

Kathy, Michael and I moved into a rented cabin on Leech Lake. It was only a couple miles from Ah-Gwah-Ching. The front windows faced east over frozen Shingobee Bay. Each day, right around supper time, we'd watch Michael climb up a kitchen chair so he could see the train rumbling over the trestle that stretched across the bay. He'd look at us and point out the window. And then he'd express his excitement in a gleeful language that only he understood. I think I knew what he meant, because I felt the same way.

Each day at work it seemed that I was learning something new about vending machines. Unlike the classroom setting, where the equipment was empty, these machines had real money and real product in them. The water in the coffee machines was hot enough to burn me. The sugar would make a real mess if I didn't pour it into its canister just right. Coins, which belonged to real customers, would get jammed in the changers and my bookkeeping no longer dealt with an imaginary business.

In mid June, a letter arrived from the Business Enterprise Program announcing a new business that was to open in September. It was located in Grand Rapids, an hour's drive from Walker. The letter described an all-vending-machine business located on the campus of Itasca Community College.

Combining relaxed summer hours with a great place to raise kids, I saw no other option. I wrote my letter. Someone higher on the seniority list could take the new enterprise before I'd even see it, but you never know. Nothing ventured, nothing gained, I thought as I took it to the mail box. Now the only thing left to do was wait for a phone call telling me that it was my turn to look at the new business.

A couple weeks passed and my phone remained quiet. Finally, I called Mr. Hamilton to see if he knew anything. He told me that there were five interested vendors on the list. Each one had more seniority than I did.

"However," he said, "two have already changed their minds."

"Why?" I asked, almost in disbelief.

"One didn't say; the other turned it down for health reasons. When he found out that there would be some heavy lifting involved with all the canned pop, he decided not to look at it."

Choosing to be hopeful, I started thinking about some of the things I'd need to know if I were to move to Grand Rapids. I made a list of questions to ask about the new business. The list was short to begin with. I wrote down things like: what about storage areas, telephone service, and what about a coin counter? With each new day came a new question.

Finally, one day near the end of July, Fran Bussey, Jr., BEP supervisor of the northeast district, called me with the news that I was next on the list. We set up a time when Kathy and I and Chuk Hamilton could meet in Grand Rapids and look at the business.

Two days later, Mr. Bussey met us in the staff parking lot to begin our campus tour. Our first stop was the administration building to meet Cricket Guyer and Will Backes, my campus contacts, and then we continued through the six buildings where we had vending machines.

The four of us stood outside Mullins Hall after our campus tour. A warm, but gusty wind whistled through the white pines.

"Well, Mr. Miller," Mr. Bussey spoke. "What do you think?"

"I believe I'll take it! Where is the paperwork? I'm ready to sign."

"I have it right here." He opened his briefcase. "Before you sign the contract, do you have any questions?"

"Oh, that's right," I said, "I have them right here." Reaching into my jacket pocket, I pulled out my list, which, by that time had become quite long. It flapped in the breeze as we discussed each point. When we completed the list, I signed the contract. School was starting in a few days and seventeen vending machines needed to be filled!

Chapter 16

"Faster Daddy, Faster"

On June 15, 1982, I became a father once again. This time, the little bundle with long dark hair was a beautiful baby girl. Arms that hugged, held and wrestled with a two-and-a-half-year-old boy, now trembled when I held Lindsey. She made our family complete.

It was after dark when we pulled into the driveway in front of my folks' house. Michael, four years old, was the first out of the car, excited to see his grandparents. The summer air was cool and moist, tossed by a southern breeze. In the distance, the new bug zapper was doing its job and the river was quietly brushing the shoreline.

By the time Kathy and I had unloaded the car, Michael had already told Grandma about our drive. Then his attention was drawn to the bright light and snapping sound that came from the back yard. Grandma explained that the bugs were attracted to the light and then, when they got real close, they would be zapped.

Running across the living room floor to where I stood, he grabbed my hand and pulled me toward the picture window on the other side of the room.

"Daddy, Daddy, come see the bug zappu!"

"It's too far away for Daddy to see," I said.

He was quiet for a moment, and then said, "Den yissen Daddy, yissen."

I had been keeping track of the weekly sales figures from each of my 21 vending machines by using thirteen column ledger paper, my glasses, a felt tip pen and a calculator equipped with a large-number display. Some machines were subject to sales tax, some were not. Some were subject to commissions and some were not. My calculations could easily cover an entire page and those pages could get quite messy.

Handwriting my monthly reports to the Business Enterprise Program was becoming tedious so I decided to explore the possibility of using a computer to take care of all my bookkeeping needs.

Curious, but not knowing the first thing about computers, I stopped by the campus computer lab and tried to read some text on the screen with my glasses. Their high level of magnification pulled the pixels apart leaving a flickering blur. I needed some software that would make the images on the screen large so my glasses would become unnecessary.

I started asking people on campus who were computer users if they new anything about any screen-enlargement programs. I learned that several were available, but they were all pretty pricey; one was nearly two thousand dollars, just for the software. I'd need to sell quite a few Snickers to see that kind of money.

Then, one day over lunch, I was talking to Bob Schwob, one of the biology teachers on campus, about my computer conundrum.

"Wait a minute," he said thoughtfully. "I think I have something like that on my Macintosh. It comes bundled with some other system software."

"You mean it's free?" I asked trying to hold back the hope.

"Yes." he said. "It's included in the price of the Mac. Stop by my office after three and we'll take a look."

That afternoon I walked into his office in Wilson hall. He was sitting at his computer.

"I found what you're looking for." he said. "It's called CloseView." He stood up from his chair. "Here, have a seat."

Sitting in the chair, I faced the screen. "This is when CloseView is off," he said. Squinting at the small screen in front of me, I could barely tell that there was anything visible, let alone readable.

"Now," he said, pressing a couple keys. "Do you see that empty black box in the middle of the screen?"

"Yes. I do." I could feel myself getting excited.

136

"When the magnification is turned on, the whole screen will be filled with whatever is inside of that black box. To move the magnified area, just move the mouse. You can adjust the amount of magnification by using the command, option and arrow keys."

He hit a couple more keys and I found myself staring at letters that were three inches high! Only one or two words and two or three lines could be seen at a time, but there they were and I could read.

"I have a meeting to attend and then I'm going home. Turn the machine off and close the door when you are finished."

With that he was gone and it was just me and Mac. I stayed and played for an hour and a half. This much fun, I thought, should not be legal.

Over the next weeks I learned how to use the Mac and then ordered my own. With Bob's help and some cassette teaching guides I borrowed from my dad, I learned to use word processing, database and spreadsheet programs. Within the next six months I was sending computer-generated reports to St. Paul.

Mike and Lindsey were six and four when Kathy went back to school to complete her degree in elementary education. Almost all her classes were held in the evenings or on weekends. Up to that point, Kathy was the one who read the kids bedtime stories. Now, with her in school, it was my turn.

By this time, we had assembled quite a library of Bible story books and children's literature. Our bookshelves were filled with everything from Joseph and His Colorful Coat to The Cat in the Hat. The kids had their favorites, but I wasn't ready to put them through the agony of listening to me read. So, instead of *reading* them the stories, I decided to *tell* them the stories.

To keep their attention, I tried to make the stories as contemporary as possible. For instance, in the story of David and Goliath, when Jesse sent David with food, to visit his brothers on the battle line, David rode his BMX bike to McDonald's drive-through and then continued to the valley of Ella!

In the story of Elijah and the prophets of Baal, we thought up some other reasons for Elijah to give to the prophets to explain why their god was not answering their prayers. The best answer, as far as Mike and Lindsey were concerned, was that Baal was probably in the bathroom and could not hear their cries for help.

And of course we can't forget the King and the Mystery Man. Crossing my arms on my chest and scowling, I'd begin the story: Nebuchadnezzar had a problem. Three young men in his kingdom were not obeying his rules. They weren't worshiping the idol he had made and that made him mad.

"Make the furnace seven times hotter than usual," snarled the king to his guards. "That'll teach 'em to disobey ME!."

After the guards threw Shadrach, Meshach and Abednego into the fiery furnace, the king couldn't resist peaking inside. Blinking his eyes, he counted. And then he counted again."

"Didn't you toss three men into the blaze?" he demanded of his guards.

"Yes, sir," They shouted. "We threw three into the furnace!"

"Why, then, do I count FOUR?"

Stopping the story, I'd ask the kids: "Who was the fourth man?" I hardly had time to finish the question when they would shout, in unison: "Jesus!"

After all the fun was over, prayers were said and they were tucked in, I'd walk down the hall to the living room and sit on the couch. My prayer for them was, and still is, that when they get into their own "fiery furnace," they will know they are not alone.

Snow crunched under my boots as I made my way down the river bank to the frozen Crow Wing. The sky above me was white as was the ground beneath me. Dark silhouettes, that I knew to be trees, stood quietly on each side of the river dividing land and sky. Their undefined outlines looked as if someone had dragged a huge piece of charcoal from east to west.

Far off in the distance I could hear the buzz of a snowmobile and happy voices. Dad, Mike and Lindsey had gone to the garage to get the snowmobile and toboggan for a ride on the river. As they grew closer, so did the sound of Lindsey's laughter.

Stopping a few feet from where I stood, Lindsey called to me from her seat behind Grandpa, "C'mon, Daddy, it's fun!" I took my position behind Mike on the sled, crossing my legs and grabbing the ropes threaded along its sides. Grandpa gunned the throttle and our toboggan caught the edge of a snow drift that threw a bucket load of snow in my face. Our ride had begun!

We zipped upstream to where the Leaf River empties into the Crow Wing. The river bed was quite wide at that point and that made it a good place to turn around. Grandpa didn't decrease speed on the turn and our sled gained momentum as we swung in a wide arch behind the speeding machine.

Our toboggan seemed to fly as it glanced off the tops of the snow drifts. Mike and I leaned hard to the left and clung to our ropes to keep us from being tossed onto the crusty snow like two tumbling tumbleweeds!

On the return trip, Grandpa seemed to find every snow drift on the river. Once he spotted one, he'd drive the snowmobile just close enough so that our toboggan hit it straight on. Each time we smashed into one of those moveable mounds, our laughing mouths were filled with snow and our smiling eyes were blinded by an explosion of chilly white.

Mike and I managed to maintain our tight grip on the toboggan as we raced back down stream. But then, unexpectedly, Dad slowed the snowmobile down, stopped and turned the engine off. We slid to a crunchy halt a few feet behind him and waited.

Getting off the machine, he walked back to where we sat and asked me a question that caught me completely by surprise, "Do you want to drive for a while?"

For a moment I didn't know what to say or how to respond. Of course I'd like to drive. But I hadn't even thought it was possible. But Dad had been thinking. "The river bed is frozen solid," he continued, "and there are no stumps or ice ridges that you could run into. All you have to do is keep it between the trees."

"C'mon, Daddy, let's go!" Lindsey was eager to get moving again.

"Give it a try, Dad." Mike's tone was a bit more cautious than his sister's.

"Just keep it on the white between the trees and you'll be fine. I'll ride with Mike until we get home. Then I'll go get the camera and you can take the kids around the island in front of the house."

"C'mon, Daddy!" Lindsey could hardly sit still.

Dad turned the key and the snowmobile came alive. I threw my leg across the chugging machine and listened to Dad explain the throttle, brakes and how to steer. I looked up through the windshield and thought to myself, "I can do this!" It reminded me of playing one of those race car video games at the arcade, the type that has a steering wheel and the object of the game is to stay on the road. Tightening my grip on the throttle, the machine grew noisy and moved forward. Slowly at first, but soon we were traveling down that wide white road at a comfortable speed. Chomping my cheek, I thought, "I could get used to this." When the black smudge I knew to be the island in front of my folks' house came into view, I stopped the machine so Dad could get off and go get the camera.

My first trip around the island was tentative. I wanted to get an idea of what it was like before increasing speed. Lindsey's mitten-covered finger kept poking me in the ribs as she called out, "Faster, Daddy, faster!" I twisted the throttle on her request a couple times, but soon realized that her enthusiasm for higher speeds was far greater than my ability to stay in control of that mighty machine. Alone on the toboggan, Mike was air born, even at moderate speeds.

We had made several trips around the island when I thought I heard my name. Slowing the machine and looking to the right, I could make out a Dad shape on the river. He was waving his arms vigorously over his head trying to get my attention.

"Did you see that open water at the end of the island?" he asked.

"No. What open water?"

"It's at the end of the island, just as you turn."

Giving the machine a little gas, I approached the black blur. It was about three feet wide and nearly six feet long. Several of the tracks that we had made were within inches of the hole. Once again, a mitten-covered digit dug into my ribs.

"C'mon, Daddy! Let's go some more! And this time, Daddy, let's go faster!"

Chapter 17

A Competent Question

Air brakes hissed as we turned into the Minneapolis Greyhound Depot. A bit groggy from my four and a half hour ride, I started to come alive when the door opened; the bus began to fill with muggy summer air. I was in town for a business meeting at the SSB office in St. Paul.

Exiting the depot, past the panhandlers, I headed straight for a familiar street corner. From there, it was a short walk to Nicollet Avenue. Turning left on Nicollet, with the sun on my back, I'd follow it to Fourth and catch a 16A to my hotel. The route was familiar and this time of year there were no piles of snow to impede my progress.

But today, something was different. Something was not right. Instead of being greeted by honking horns and squealing tires, I was surrounded by gear-grinding dump trucks and growling bulldozers. The air around me was not filled with car exhaust; it smelled like my uncle's freshly-tilled garden.

A few more steps and I stood at a familiar corner. But instead of the grayish blur that I would assume to be the street, the smeared swath in front of me was dark. The road was gone!

Standing by the curb, wondering what to do next, a deep voice cut through my confusion.

"Hey man, have you got some spare change? We're savin' up for bus fare to get back home."

I avoided his question with one of my own, "What's all the noise?"

"Oh, man, they're tearin' up the road!"

Road construction? How am I going to get to Nicollet now? My neat and clean plan was being dug up by the dozers. My mind was racing to find a solution when his voice interrupted my problem solving once again.

"Hey, man, have you got some spare change?"

Turning to face him, I noticed another people-shape had joined us. The second shape was tall and said nothing. I was about to snap at them, out of my new found frustration, when a thought occurred to me.

"Yes, I have some spare change," I said, "and it's yours if you can get me to Nicollet Avenue."

"No problem. It's right this way." I took one of them by the elbow and we headed for the other end of the block.

The route that they chose led away from the direction that I thought we should be going. Stumbling through shallow furrows and tripping over piles of dirt, I started to wonder if this was a good idea. I looked up to see if the buildings were getting taller, which meant we were heading toward downtown. The buildings were getting shorter.

The sound of the heavy equipment was muffled by the buildings and I had no idea where I was. The only thing I did know was that I was with two big men that I had met outside the bus depot and they knew where they could find some spare change.

Without warning the man whose elbow I was holding stopped and shook my hand from his arm.

"Look man," he said, "you're killin' me with that grip. I got to have blood flowin' in my arm. You wanna go to Nicollet and that's where we're goin'. Now relax!"

Relieved and embarrassed, I took his elbow again and we resumed our journey. Twenty steps later we were once again on hard pavement and after one more block they announced that we were now on Nicollet Avenue. Sheepishly I dug some change out of my pocket and gave it to them. They disappeared into the crowd.

Turning my back to the sun, I continued my trek to Fourth.

My brother, Doug, was working for The Daily Plainsman, the newspaper in Huron, South Dakota. He helped with the final layout of the paper before it went to press. While he enjoyed his job, it often kept him from getting back to Staples for holidays.

Sometimes, my youngest brother, Jon, would drive out to spend time with him. Since Doug did not keep his fridge full, eating out was always on the agenda. On their way down the stairs from Doug's apartment to find a restaurant, something caught Jon's eye.

"Hey, Doug."

"Yeah?"

"How'd you get that bump? Bang your head on a kitchen cupboard, or what?"

"I dunno," he reached up and felt the top of his head. "It's probably nothin'."

A few days later our phone rang.

In a voice that tried to be confident, Mom told us that the lump was malignant. "It's definitely the 'C word.'"

"How's he doing?" I asked, trying to sound strong.

Her voice trembled. "He says he can beat it. Between prayer and treatment, he says he can beat it."

Stunned, I returned the phone to its cradle. This is not right, I thought. This sort of thing does not happen to a thirty-two-year-old man. My brother shouldn't be sick. He's never hurt anyone. It's just not right.

My Saturday morning sleep-in was interrupted by a grumpy northwest wind pushing and shoving its way between our house and garage. Tugging the warm blanket up over my head, I strained to imagine July sunshine spilling through the window. Winter was dragging on much, much too long and I was feeling a bit grumpy myself.

Physical exercise is good for putting cabin fever on the run, I reasoned, and we did have a family membership at the Itasca County YMCA. Maybe I should go over there and run the track and lift some weights. That should cheer me up.

I sat up in bed and was about to wake Kathy and ask her if she would take me to the "Y," when I remembered our conversation at dinner last night. In that conversation she had told me of the difficult week she'd had at work. Personality conflicts and misunderstandings among staff members had added pressure to her work days. Her evenings had been filled with meetings and teachers' conferences. Being the only driver in the family, her late afternoons were spent getting groceries, taking me on business errands and getting the kids to piano lessons on time. Kathy is a master organizer and model of efficiency, but at this point, she was completely exhausted and the last thing in the world she needed was for me to wake her up and tell her that I needed a ride to the "Y" because I was feeling a little grumpy.

If I had a driver's license, I'd drive myself. If I could see, I'd be doing more of the errands and she could spend more time doing what she wanted to do, not taking us where we needed to go. It bothered me every time she had to take the car to do something that I should be doing. Every couple that I knew shared the responsibilities of being the family "taxi". Why should we have to be different?

I spent the next few moments juggling transportation ideas around in my head but could not find a solution to my problem. I recalled the freedom I felt when we lived in Fargo. I could walk to almost any location I wanted to in the downtown area. I didn't even have to arrange rides for work. It was as simple as walking down a few flights of stairs. Living in Fargo was uncomplicated freedom and I loved it!

As I contemplated my predicament, I began to get in touch with some powerful and ugly feelings about being blind. Like a man confronted by thugs in a dark alley, I knew I would have to fight if I explored those feelings any further. Then I heard the click. Someone had opened a switchblade. The fight was on!

The first thrust cut the rope around Pandora's Box and the lid flew open.

I was tired of having to make arrangements for transportation. I was tired of being blind when most of my friends were not. I was tired of the awkward way my blindness made others feel. I was tired of answering the question, "How much can you see?" I was tired of trying to "roll with the punches". I wanted to do some "punching" of my own!

In the small fellowship that we were attending, responsibility for the Sunday morning message was shared by several of the men—and it was my turn.

Recently I had been struck by the contrast between the way our culture defines strength and the way God defines it in His Son, the Lamb that was slain. My six pages of large print notes were stapled together to keep them in order. Paper clips attached to pages in my Bible would help me find scripture references quickly and easily.

Scanning the room, I guessed that we had from forty to fifty people-shapes in the service that summer morning. Since that was more than our usual number, I assumed we had visitors. After the songs and testimonies, I stood to my feet and took my place behind the music stand we used as a pulpit. After welcoming our guests, I opened with prayer, then asked everyone to turn in their Bibles to Revelation, Chapter Five.

My Bible was already opened to the right spot so I put on my glasses, lifted it to my face, stuck my nose on the page and started to read. When I finished reading I put the Bible on the music stand, took off my glasses and picked up my large print notes. It was then that I heard a shuffling and rustling of books and papers. I interpreted the noise and moving shapes at the back of the room as people, several people, getting up and leaving.

When the meeting was over I asked Gari Smith if she had talked to the folks that had been in the back row.

"Yes, I did. They said that they were passing through town and were looking for the 'faith church.' They said this sure wasn't it."

I knew what they meant by that remark. A blind man would never have been permitted to speak at a "faith church" unless he had been healed.

I remembered the time I had come home from work to find an old friend had dropped in and was talking to Kathy about her new understanding of what "faith" really was. She had been there for a couple of hours and was just then on her way to the door.

When I walked into the house she turned to me and said, "Ken Miller, you've given up on being healed. If you would just take hold of faith, God would heal you!" I stepped aside and held the door for her as she passed. As the door closed, I wished it were as easy as she made it sound.

When we stepped out of the hotel we were greeted by a smothering curtain of oppressive humidity and the din of traffic. Elevated trains clattered above us and taxi horns were screaming all around us. It seemed everything was racing at top speed, including the folks on the sidewalk.

I was in Chicago with two other blind businessmen from Minnesota. Curt Jones, Jim Duit and I represented our state at a series of meetings related to the Randolf-Sheppard vending program. We had just returned from an afternoon session when Curt had an idea.

"Hey, Ken, let's go shopping. I want to get a souvenir for Daniel before they tear down Comiskey Park."

"Sounds good to me. Let's do it."

"I think Jim wants to come, too. He said he'd meet us here after he puts his notes in his room."

Just then, there was a knock at the door and Jim walked in. White cane in hand and a smile in his voice, he said, "Ready men?"

"Ready as we'll ever be!" Curt's cane clacked as he opened it.

I opened mine too and we headed for the elevator.

Once in the lobby we stopped at the front desk and told the clerk we wanted to pick up some souvenirs and wondered if he could give us directions.

"Certainly, gentlemen. Our hotel gift shop is right around the corner at the other end of this desk."

"No, not the hotel gift shop," Curt protested. "We are looking for a sport shop where I could get a souvenir from Comiskey Park."

"Sport shop," the clerk said thoughtfully. "Ah-umm, just take a right out the front door and go to the end of this block." He continued, "Then turn left, cross the street, keep going for two blocks and it's the shop on the corner. They may have what you are looking for."

Thanking him, we headed for the door. Curt took my elbow and Jim held onto Curt's. Once outside, we jumped into the river of pedestrians that was rushing past. Our shopping trip had begun.

We had no trouble finding the shop. It was right where the clerk had directed us. However, they did not have what we were looking for. The young man behind the counter told us that there was a sport shop in a nearby mall that might stock items from Comiskey Park. He gave us directions and we were off once again.

After crossing several streets and turning several corners, I started to get concerned because there was no mall. I thought I had followed his directions to the letter, but we found ourselves at a busy street corner that had no stop lights. We stood there wondering what to do when a woman's voice sliced through the din around us.

"Where are you guys going?"

"We need to get to the sport shop that's in a mall somewhere around here," I shouted over the roar of a passing bus.

"I work in that mall. It's right across the street. Take my elbow and I'll get you there. The traffic is pretty crazy and we'll have to hurry, so when I say go--I mean go!"

Curt already had my elbow and Jim had Curt's. Endless traffic blew dust in our faces as we waited.

"Go!" We were off like a pack of hounds at the raceway. I almost lost my grip as she bolted towards the other side of the street. "Step up!" she yelled as we reached the curb. A few steps later and we were in the quiet calm of the mall.

This mall was not one of those new-construction-everything-in-a-row type malls. No, it was one of those converted warehouse types. You know the kind I mean, shops of all shapes with staircases in weird places, glass display cases in the middle of angled walkways. No doubt the unorthodox layout and glint of polished banisters create a scene that is visually appealing, but to someone with little or no vision, getting around in one of these lovely labyrinths can be a navigational nightmare!

"Which shop are you looking for?" she asked.

"The sport shop." Curt said.

"Okay. It's right up here."

A few steps later and we were standing in front of an open door.

"Here we are, guys, I have to get back to work. See ya!"

And she was gone.

"Can I help you?" A voice came from inside the shop.

"Yes," Curt responded. "What sort of souvenirs do you have from Comiskey Park?"

"The only items we have right now are a poster and a commemorative coin. Are you interested in either of those?"

"No thanks."

"We expect more in a couple days," he added.

For the second time that day, we were unable to find the right souvenir.

"It's getting late," I commented. "We better get back to the hotel."

"Sounds good. Which way do we go, Mr. Miller?" Curt asked.

Surveying our surroundings, I realized I had no idea how to get to the exit. Ahead of me, I could make out three possible aisles. I opted for the widest one and it led us right to the staircase that took us to the street.

Humid air filled our lungs and traffic noise filled our ears as we left the mall and headed for the street corner. Rush hour had kicked into high gear and the noise made it impossible to discern whether it was safe to cross the street in any direction.

"Keep walking?" I shouted.

"Yup!"

The next corner was equipped with a light so we waited for it to change and we were on our way.

Our return trip was going smoothly until something in the distance did not look right. The gray trail of fog, that I knew to be the sidewalk, disappeared about fifteen feet ahead of us.

"I think we might be in trouble men," I said.

"Why, what's wrong?"

"It looks like the sidewalk ends up here. We may have to turn around and go a different way."

"You mean we're lost?" Curt pretended panic and then turned to Jim. "See, Jim, I told ya. This is just the sort of thing that happens when you go shopping with a blind guy."

We took a few more steps forward and stopped. Was that kielbasa wafting passed my nose? Or was it pepperoni? Then I heard hushed conversation and the clink of silverware on plates. We were not at a dead end; we were at a sidewalk cafe. Following that narrow ribbon of gray between the tables could get us to the other side.

Slowly we approached the cluster of tables. I entered the passageway that looked like it would get us through. As we moved toward the other end of the cafe, I could hear chairs being moved as customers cleared the path for us. Our confidence grew as we made our way to the other side. So far, we had not bumped a table, chair or even a waiter! We were almost to the end of the path when I heard something thud and crunch as it hit the sidewalk.

"Keep moving," Curt whispered. "It wasn't us, I hope!"

Two hours after we left on our shopping trip, we stood, empty handed, in the lobby of our hotel.

"What do we do now, men?" I asked. "We didn't get a single souvenir."

Curt was the first to offer a suggestion. "The hotel gift shop is right around the corner at the end of the front desk."

It was almost time for babysitting to begin. Not children, vending machines. Before the advent of computerized coin mechanisms, anyone who operated vending machines had to wrestle with their mechanical predecessors. With so

148

many moving parts, trouble was often just a bent nickel away. No matter how much training an operator had, no matter how skilled you were as a technician, it was impossible to prevent these mechanical marvels from breaking down or jamming up.

Three canned pop, one snack, one pastry, one coffee and one sandwich machine formed a line against the west wall of the cafeteria and odds were good that one or more of them would act up during lunch. Therefore, I spent the lunch hours babysitting.

I had just entered the cafeteria when I heard a familiar voice.

"Hey, Ken..." The voice belonged to Jim Gabrielsen, one of the psychology instructors on campus. "There's room at this table, come join me for lunch." I could always count on his upbeat personality and positive attitude toward life to keep lunch lively. We engaged in many non-combative discussions about politics, religion and current events. Sometimes the discussion would come around to my blindness.

Today's puzzler caught me completely by surprise.

"Where do you feel most competent, at work or at home?"

"What do you mean? Competent?"

"Where do you feel the most capable when it comes to mechanical things?"

When he asked me the second time, I understood exactly what he meant. I was just about to purchase an electric garage door opener, and I didn't know anything about their operation or installation. We were finding puddles of water on our basement floor under the upstairs shower and the back door to our house didn't close as it should. These were all tasks that, I assumed, the man of the house should deal with.

Secretly, I dreaded the thought of tackling these projects. I feared that they would end in failure. Then I'd have to call in a professional and feel like an idiot. But at the same time, when it came to leaky valves, jammed coins, jammed pop cans or clogged mixing bowls, I knew exactly what to do.

"I feel most competent at work."

"I thought you might. I don't think your competence has anything to do with your ability. I think you feel more competent at work because someone showed you what to do. If you had the same kind of 'hands on' training for home repair, that you did for machine repair, you'd feel the same level of competence whether you were at home or at work. The issue is not ability; the issue is education."

He was right. Two months later, with some instruction and supervision from Jim Davis, I put a laundry tub and bathroom sink in our basement. Much to my surprise, it wasn't that difficult.

Chapter 18

Seeing Isn't Believing

Insects buzzed in the fields outside the Iowa farm house. Occasionally, a hungry one would bounce off the screen door that separated the kitchen from the porch. Hot summer sun had driven the temperature to almost ninety degrees that day and we all wished we had gone into town to the pool. Our friend Patti Sandberg had just arrived home from her new job and we were all sitting around the supper table trying to figure out how to spend the evening when the phone rang. Patti answered it.

"Ken, it's for you. It's your Mom."

"Doug is in the hospital," she said. "When will you be back to Minnesota?"

Recently Doug had not been doing well in his fight against cancer. He had been wrestling the killer for the past five years and his attitude was always positive, even as he lost his hair to chemotherapy.

Watching his struggle was like living on a roller coaster. The cancer would go into remission and we'd all rejoice. Then it would come back and we'd all be depressed. Doug would be down about its return for a couple days and then he'd grit his teeth saying, "I'm gonna beat this thing", and go back to his newspaper job. But, like repeated blows from an ax that can bring down the sturdiest oak, repeated returns of the killer was grinding his endurance to sawdust.

Each summer my dad loads his Harley Davidson onto a trailer and takes it to Rapid City, South Dakota. From there, a biker could spend endless days riding through the Black Hills. Mom and we three sons took turns going with him. Seeing a change in Doug's health, Dad decided to break the rotation. Doug's doctors said it might be the last time Doug could take such a trip, but, nevertheless, plans could be made. To prepare, Doug had a blood transfusion and some serious chemotherapy. On the day Dad picked him up, one of his co-workers said Doug had a spring in his step like he did before he got sick.

Even though the cancer continued to rage in his body, Doug enjoyed every minute of the trip. Less than two hours after Dad dropped him off at Huron, he called Staples to say that he was really sick. Three days later he entered the St. Cloud hospital.

I was not prepared for what I saw when I walked into his room. Following Kathy to his bedside, I greeted him and looked intently at the blur that I knew was my brother. Something was wrong. He was bald. I hated the way the room smelled; I hated the way he looked! Oh God, I thought, why don't you come down here and heal this man? He never hurt anyone. He's never done anything to deserve this! This is not just! He is only 37! Angry tears began to form in my eyes.

Then a nurse came into the room and told us she had to change the bedding so we walked out into the waiting room. I wanted to hit someone. I wanted to scream; I wanted to cry. Dad told us that the staff at the hospital said Doug was an excellent patient. Doug may be an excellent patient, I thought, but he shouldn't be a patient at all.

Once back in his room, we started talking about his computer and the new graphics software he had just installed. Then he told me about all the things he was going to do when he gets back to work. Gets back to work? The words screamed in my ears. Doesn't he know? Doesn't he know he's not going back to work?

Two days later the phone rang and Mom told me my brother was dead. The previous summer, we had attended my sister-in-law Carolyn's funeral. Now it was time to attend Doug's.

At his wake, my brother Jon and I stood over Doug's casket and reminisced. I reached out and touched Doug's abdomen where the tumor had been. The basketball-sized lump was gone. I took twisted pleasure in knowing the thing that had killed my brother was, at last, dead, too.

Early morning summer sunshine poured in our picture window, warming the carpet under my feet. Afternoon temps would surely send us to the lake. A quick lunch after church, and we'd be on our way.

We arrived just as everyone was getting settled in their seats. That morning we had a guest speaker who would be preaching.

"This is good," I thought. "Guests always bring something new. What will it be?"

As he began his message, however, my curiosity turned to apprehension. His topic was faith and receiving answers to prayer. I knew what would happen after his message.

It had been several years since I had stood in a healing line. I had left that whole subject in God's hands. Now I was confronted with it once again.

Questions immediately began to flood my mind. Is this going to be the same type of message about faith I have heard for the past twenty years? Or will this man have some new thoughts? I have not been healed yet, will he somehow know the reason why? Do I dare believe again? Is this the man that God will use to bring healing to me?

I did not know the answers to those questions. But I could feel my insides tighten up and that unmistakable burning sensation in my nose. Oh God, I prayed, I want to see!

When he read the words of Jesus saying, "Ask and you will receive", my throat dried up; it hurt to swallow. He told of miracles in his own family that were supernatural. God had done it for him. He told us God could do it for us, too. His message of hope went on for twenty minutes or so. It was filled with scriptures, personal experiences and exhortations. I knew that at the end he would ask anyone who wanted prayer to come to the front of the church. What was I going to do then?

My head was filled with a chorus of voices, all attempting to give me advice. First to speak was History, "Tough to call. You have been prayed for so many times, I've lost track and your eyesight is still the same." Next to speak was Pragmatic, with a touch of cynicism, "Don't bother. You've been prayed for by some big name evangelists and it didn't help. What makes you think this man's prayers will be any different?" Then Spiritual countered with," Wait a minute, Pragmatic, it's God who does the healing, not man. Ken, I say you go for it!" Then Excitement joined in, "Yes, go for it! This could be God's time to heal you! You don't want to miss your opportunity; this may be your last chance! Don't blow it! Ask and keep on asking!"

At the end of his message he invited anyone who wanted prayer to come to the front of the church. A line of around fifteen people shapes began to form. I turned to Kathy to see if she had any insight for me. I knew she understood my dilemma.

Decision time had come. What should I do? Did I want to be vulnerable again? Did I want to bring my request to the Creator of the Universe and run the risk of being denied one more time? Or should I stay safe and remain seated? Kathy squeezed my hand and smiled, "I'm with you whatever you decide."

Again, I struggled with what to do. "I can't just sit here," I thought. "What if this is the time for me to be healed? What if I sit here and do nothing and miss God's will for me?" Finally, I silenced all the voices of reason and excitement and made my decision. I swallowed to clear my throat, blinked to clear my eyes, stood to my feet and walked down the aisle.

Starting with the folks at the other end of the line, his approach was simple and unemotional. He asked each person why they had come for prayer and then prayed for them. Nothing dramatic, just honest prayers from a sincere man. Several of the people he had prayed for were weeping. It was obvious that there were many tender hearts in that line.

The closer he came to me, the tighter the knot inside me became. My body was beginning to tremble as he grew near. Not just a little, but a lot. I thought I would lose my balance and fall over. I wanted to see. I wanted to be healed.

By the time he reached me, the trembling was so intense I could hardly speak. He put his left hand on my shoulder and asked me what I wanted prayer for. I managed to stop shaking long enough to force words from my stammering lips, "I am almost blind; I want to see."

I closed my eyes as he placed his right hand on my head and prayed. "Lord, may that same Spirit that raised Christ Jesus from the dead come and heal these eyes, in Jesus' name, amen."

A moment later I opened my eyes. Nothing had changed. Feeling like a chump who had been sucker punched, I made my way to the back of the church where Kathy was waiting for me. She took my hand as we left the building. Mike and Lindsey were already waiting for us in the van.

Once again I asked God why. Why wasn't I healed? Everything he had said, everything he had read from the Bible, all the personal experiences he had shared pointed to a wonderful healing for me. Why didn't it happen? Had I somehow been at fault? Did I do something wrong? Didn't I have enough faith? Maybe I just didn't believe hard enough.

In an instant, I was aware of other voices joining my own as I fought to find some sort of answer that would bring me some peace. These new voices were challenging the very foundation of my faith in God and my relationship with Jesus. Like crazed chain saws, they ripped and chewed at the roots of everything I knew to be true.

My emotions came alive as the taunting grew more intense. "God doesn't really love you! If he did, you would be healed by now! Why do you go on with this God stuff anyway? It doesn't work. That man lied to you. Everyone has lied to you! It's all a lie. God is dead, or haven't you heard? The Bible is just a bunch of empty promises. You're never going to get healed! Give it up! Get bitter, you have every right to get bitter! If Jesus really meant what he said about ask and you will receive, you would have your sight and your brother wouldn't be dead! Come on, get smart, get bitter!"

For a moment, I thought I was losing my mind. I tried to hold my ground against the swarm of angry, buzzing bees, but my weary will and fragile faith were truly damaged.

Crippled in the midst of it all, I could almost hear the confused voice of John the Baptist crying out from his prison cell to his cousin, Jesus, "Are you the one? Or should I look for another?"

When we walked through the back door of our house, I could smell the baked chicken dinner that was waiting for us. Kathy had set the oven timer to turn on while we were away. Everyone ate except me. I wasn't hungry.

After dinner, Kathy and I went to the living room to talk about the morning. I needed to unload. Sitting on the couch, I told her about my thoughts and feelings during each part of the service.

When I told her I thought I might miss my opportunity for healing if I didn't respond to the prayer line, she asked me this question, "Do you perceive God as an all powerful "tease" who dangles a carrot in front of you, only to yank it away when you reach for it?"

My first thought was to protest her assertion and sputter something like, "Of course not! God would never do such a thing!" But I had to be honest with myself. Her question was a good one. It was insightful and sharp as a fresh razor. It cut past the outer layers of "goodness" and "correct answers" and exposed a hidden judgment that, even I didn't know existed.

She was right. I didn't want to admit it, but she was right. I believed, intellectually, that God was not a tease, yet at the same time, I couldn't deny what I now saw was true. I did feel teased. It was always fun hearing how others received their "carrots", but when it came my turn, for some reason, my "carrot" was always out of reach.

"Today," I sighed, "I felt teased, even betrayed. It made me crazy. I know God can do it. He did it when Jesus was on earth. Why not now? I've asked so many times, and the result is always the same. It's a mystery to me."

"Since your healing is such a mystery, why do you keep going for prayer? Sometimes I think your sanity is on the line. It's almost like you're beating yourself up every time you stand in a healing line."

"I can't help it. I want to see! I have to keep on asking."

"But it's going to drive you nuts. It's going to kill your faith." Then she stopped and looked at me. "Ken," she paused, "you are blind."

"Of course I am, but God can..."

A flash of movement told me she had raised her hand like a policeman stopping traffic. "No buts. You are blind."

I looked at her, puzzled by her words. "You are blind," she said again.

"B-L-I-N-D! And there is nothing you can do about it. You can try all the formulas, you can beg and plead with God, you can try to manipulate him with Bible verses, but I do not believe that being healed is your greatest need. I believe your greatest need is to find a place of rest and peace about your blindness. Until you find that rest and accept your blindness, you will continue to beat yourself up searching for your miracle."

Her words were filled with love, but like the arrow from an expert archer's bow, their truth hit a painful bull's eye. I put my head in my hands and wept. My weeping turned to sobbing as years of disappointment, frustration and anger poured from my innermost being. There were no words to convey my sadness. No words to express the sorrow I felt.

"Jesus," I prayed. "I can't do this anymore. If You intend to heal my optic nerves, You'll have to let me know in a real clear way: a burning bush or stone tablets with super large print would work the best. Until then, I'll be staying in my seat. Amen."

Epilogue

We pulled back from traditional church involvement, choosing instead to attend a small home group. When we did talk about divine healing, we came up with more questions than answers. After a multi-year cooling-off period, I looked at the issue again. I had, indeed, been on a collision course.

Twelve-step programs use this definition of insanity, "Insanity is doing the same thing over and over again hoping to get a different result." That was me. What kept me on the quest for my miracle? What was the hook? The hook was that I believed I had to have my sight before I could have a good life. Logic said my life was already good, but that's not where the hook was buried. The hook was buried in a belief system that would not be bothered with logic.

Whether I fashioned it with my own fins, or bought it off the shelf at Pet Palace made little difference; the fishbowl existed and my nose was shoved against it. The bowls' message was clear, "Blindness is bad. Blindness aborts a full life. If you don't have your sight, you don't have anything. A miracle is your only way out." The clear glass had become gray blocks and I needed a *get-out-of-jail-FREE* card.

Kathy's counsel to me to accept my blindness turned out to be my *card*. At first feel, it was awkward and clumsy, but soon its power was evident and comfortable. On the front of the card it said, "It's okay to be blind." When I played that card, I rejected the fishbowl and all it stands for. Once the card was on the table and it was okay to be blind, it only took one flip of my tail, and I was out of the fish bowl.

So, what about God? Do my feeble attempts at arm twisting add up to, and confirm His nonexistence? Absolutely not! Does all my fussing mean that my God is bigger than my fish bowl? Absolutely!

Acknowledgements

I could never have completed this project on my own. Here is a partial list of teammates who, by offering their expertise, made this book possible:

First, I am indebted to my parents: Mom, who aided me in keeping the beginning chapters accurate, and Dad, who made some choices early on that would ultimately lead me on a route less-traveled.

Many thanks to Guy Doud, who in 1990, gave me a "thumbs up" on my idea and told me I must write my story. Hats off to a couple of English teachers in the Grand Rapids area for offering their input and ideas on a couple of early drafts: Larry Mercier and Pat Mathias.

Also, a big thanks needs to go to a couple folks in my writers' group. To Rosalie Hunt Mellor, thanks for trying to explain to me the difference between a participle that dangles and one that doesn't. To John Michael Cook, who in addition to doing my cover illustration was a constant source of encouragement.

I am grateful to Kathy Morey, my eighth-grade English teacher at Staples High School, who proofread this manuscript and provided many needed suggestions.

Finally, I'd like to thank the folks at Trafford Publishing. In particular, thanks to Stacie Madelung for guiding me through the publishing process-so this book would find its way to you.